Led by His Love

*An Evangelical Pastor's Journey
to the Orthodox Faith*

V. REV. GORDON THOMAS WALKER

with Phillip Walker and Andrew Attaway

ANCIENT FAITH PUBLISHING

CHESTERTON, INDIANA

Published by:
   Ancient Faith Publishing
   A Division of Ancient Faith Ministries
   P.O. Box 748
   Chesterton, IN 46304

All Old Testament quotations, unless otherwise identified, are from the Orthodox Study Bible, © 2008 by St. Athanasius Academy of Orthodox Theology (published by Thomas Nelson, Inc., Nashville, Tennessee) and are used by permission. New Testament quotations are from the New King James Version of the Bible, © 1982 by Thomas Nelson, Inc., and are used by permission.

Chapter 12 was adapted in part from Fr. Gordon Walker, "What Does a Unified Orthodox Church Have to Offer America?" AGAIN, Vol. 26 no. 2, summer 2006 (a special issue devoted to Orthodox unity).

ISBN: 978-1-944967-40-6

Printed in the United States of America

Contents

Introduction 5

CHAPTER 1: Finding My Way 9

CHAPTER 2: Preacher Boy 23

CHAPTER 3: The Crash 33

CHAPTER 4: Campus Crusade 39

CHAPTER 5: Grace Haven Farm 51

CHAPTER 6: Tennessee and the NCAO 65

CHAPTER 7: Grace Valley Farm 87

CHAPTER 8: The EOC 99

CHAPTER 9: Constantinople 119

CHAPTER 10: Home at Last 131

CHAPTER 11: Being Orthodox 141

CHAPTER 12: A Vision for the Future 157

CHAPTER 13: A Final Word 165

EPILOGUE: Fond Memories 177

POSTSCRIPT: Future Plans 189

Final Thoughts 191

Introduction

THIS WORK IS THE BRAINCHILD of a group of supporters of Grace Ministries, Inc., the vehicle for accepting gifts
that Fr. Gordon founded shortly after he came to Tennessee. A
few years ago these men—all converts to Orthodoxy—spent several days at an Orthodox monastery in prayer and meditation.
On the way home, they reflected on how far they had come in
the Orthodox faith under Fr. Gordon's leadership. They decided a
book should be written about his life, both to explain his journey
and to invite others to follow into Orthodoxy.

In 2013 the board of Grace Ministries agreed with their suggestion, despite Fr. Gordon's initial hesitancy, and commissioned
Andrew Attaway, a professional Christian writer, to undertake
the project. Andrew recorded many hours of Fr. Gordon describ-
ing pivotal events in his life from birth to retirement and beyond,
and those recordings became much of the raw material for this
book. Significant contributions were also made by supporters
who had benefited from Fr. Gordon's work and wanted to share
their experiences. Andrew drafted the first portion, and I was
pleased to finish the project with input from the board and many
others.

The book explores the following issues:

1. *The growth of Fr. Gordon as he became the pastor, teacher, and leader who touched so many lives with his determined search for the New Testament church.* In addition to his quest for authentic Christian history, doctrine, and worship, Fr. Gordon felt a real need to support those with personal problems who crossed his path. Early on he developed a practice of bringing such people home for conversation, counseling if needed, and spiritual guidance when appropriate. The Walker home became well known as a place of refuge for many, especially young people, who needed a loving Christian environment and some serious spiritual help.

2. *The benefits of studying the earliest Christian Fathers' lives and writings.* Those efforts led Fr. Gordon and his colleagues from their typical Protestant beginnings to the ancient Orthodox Church. It is remarkable that these Protestants who eventually founded the Evangelical Orthodox Church (EOC) actually discovered, wrote about, and taught Orthodox doctrine and history from their own studies of the Bible and of the early church Fathers before they made contact with current canonical Orthodox leaders.

3. *The extraordinary persistence required for these believers to find an entry into canonical Orthodoxy.* When they were turned away by two major jurisdictions of the Orthodox Church, they must have felt a strong temptation to remain as the EOC and teach Orthodoxy as well as they could, making no further attempts to be canonically accepted. However, their thorough knowledge of Orthodox teachings convinced them to remain resolute and to settle for nothing less than full acceptance into the church. As Fr. Gordon explained to me, "Jesus only started one Orthodox Church."

4. *Fr. Gordon's passionate commitment to Orthodox unity*. Coming from the Protestant world, Fr. Gordon and his colleagues noted how difficult it is to explain Orthodoxy to American Protestants, Roman Catholics, or the unchurched, largely because the multiplicity of Orthodox jurisdictions causes great confusion. We who are Orthodox understand that there are no major doctrinal disagreements among jurisdictions, but the superficial differences of language and customs draw a great deal of attention away from more important issues. Fr. Gordon strongly believed Orthodoxy would flourish mightily in this country if the various jurisdictions would unite in one American Orthodox Church.

5. *The blessings Fr. Gordon and others received from Orthodoxy and the benefits they brought to Orthodoxy*. Fr. Gordon spoke often of the benefits of Orthodoxy in terms of doctrine, history, and daily practice of the faith. He strongly emphasized the assistance an experienced bishop brings to a priest and his congregation. He also noted the benefits his evangelical group brought to the Orthodox Church in North America.

It is particularly remarkable that Fr. Gordon could become so committed to the use of Orthodox liturgy, coming as he did from the Southern Baptist Convention, a denomination known for its aversion to elaborate ceremony. But he recognized both by study and by experience that the ancient Orthodox liturgy embodies a great deal of wisdom and truth in its teachings, and that its form helps to reinforce those truths.

MUCH OF THIS STORY has been recorded in other publications, but typically from the point of view of the entire group who were involved in the search for the New Testament church. This volume seeks to document the struggles, failures, and successes of one devoted Christian pastor seeking to follow the leadership of the Holy Spirit in a long and difficult journey that lasted for many years. May this small work encourage Orthodox Christians to reflect on the unique treasure of their heritage, and may it lead others to discover the ancient faith of Orthodoxy.

Fr. Gordon received ongoing assistance from a great number of parishioners, other friends, and ministerial colleagues during his career as a pastor. Many of those same believers have contributed to the story presented here. In both cases the number is too great to list everyone who assisted, even if we knew all their names. We wish to thank all who helped with Fr. Gordon's ministry and all who have contributed to this memoir, confident that God will bless those who work for the spread of His Kingdom.

Phillip Walker

CHAPTER I

Finding My Way

BY 1932, THE GREAT DEPRESSION had devastated the lives of most U.S. citizens. Twelve million Americans, almost a quarter of the workforce, were unemployed. The Depression hit hard in Birmingham, Alabama, as hard as or harder than anywhere in the country. Its steel mills were idle, and the local economy was in shambles. My father, Green Thomas Walker—G. T. to those who knew him—was grateful to be working. He was employed as a patternmaker, carving wood into molds used to cast metal machine parts, tools, and dies. At that time, he and my mother Jean had one child, one-and-a-half-year-old Alice Jean. Mother had been through a complicated labor for three days before giving birth to Alice Jean, who was born with severe physical and mental handicaps. So it was with some trepidation that they awaited their second child, thanking God when I was born healthy on April 19. Dad had been named for his father, but Mother thought Green seemed too old-fashioned, so to carry on the initials they named me Gordon Thomas.

When I was four our family moved to Palmerdale Homestead, the first of four "subsistence communities" in the Birmingham area. A project of FDR's New Deal, subsistence communities were designed to help people hit hard by the Depression. Palmerdale consisted of one hundred and four small but comfortable houses, each with a small plot of land where residents could raise their own food—their subsistence—supplementing it with whatever money they could earn. On our four-and-a-half acres we grew vegetables and kept cows, chickens, and pigs, while Dad brought in cash by patternmaking.

My dad was very patriotic and tried to enlist in the service during World War II, but his job was making molds for tank treads and hand grenades, and the recruiters thought this contribution was more important. By the end of the war he'd developed asthma from his twelve-hour shifts in the factory air, so he had to find another means of support. He was able to buy a one-third share in the Palmerdale community store and became the managing partner, running the store six days a week.

In addition to *patriotic*, another word that describes my father is *strong*. Dad could handle both hundred-pound feed sacks and ornery people.

There's a mountain east of Palmerdale called Rattlesnake Mountain. A family of moonshiners lived in a hollow behind the mountain. One of the men in the family delivered the moonshine in a truck. There was a filling station in front of Dad's store, and the moonshiner came there to buy gasoline.

One day, after two or three visits to the store for gas that week, the truck driver came to buy yet another tankful. He sauntered into the store and lazed around drinking Coke and eating cookies as usual. Dad was fed up with him, and when he started sassing Dad and cursing, Dad finally blew up. The moonshiner ended up getting a pretty good licking. He was furious when he left the store, shouting, "You can't do that to us and get by with it. We're going to kill you!"

He didn't scare Dad. "Just come over here anytime you want to have it out," Dad said. We never saw any of those moonshiners in the store again.

My mother had a strength of her own and a great deal of patience. Her first child, Alice Jean, could neither walk nor talk and required constant attention, but no one ever heard Jean Walker complain. And in addition to Alice, she had to care for me and my younger siblings David, Phillip, and Mary. Mother brought in money by selling eggs and even found the time and energy to provide meals for poorer families in the area. She would fix a dish of some kind, put us kids in the car, and drive up some little dirt road to take a family a meal. When I was delivering groceries for my dad, I drove up those same roads, and several times I got stuck, needing my dad to drive up in his truck and help me get out. I never knew how my mother could make those trips safely, but I imagined she was being looked after from above.

In most ways my boyhood was typical for our small town: hiking in the woods, climbing trees, hickory nut battles with my brother David, and exploring the hills around Palmerdale with my friends. I did get into a scrape now and then—a fight with my brother or some of the other boys in town—but the prospect of my father finding out about it was a strong deterrent. I dreamed of becoming a pilot. I loved taking care of the cows on our little farm and thought I would like to run a cattle ranch in Texas. But other influences were pulling me in a different direction.

First, there was my sister Alice. I truly loved Alice, and although she was handicapped, I always wanted her to be able to use the abilities she had. My mother told me that when Alice was five years old and I was three and a half, I tried to teach her to walk. I kept working with her till she could take a few steps. Eventually she learned to walk short distances by herself, but always needed help to walk through the house without falling.

Another important experience was our love of the church. The church was the center of our family's life, and I came to love the faith I absorbed at home and in church. I was taught several non-negotiable beliefs: (1) that the Bible was the final authority, true and trustworthy in all it teaches; (2) that you must make a decision for Christ and be born again to be saved from your sins; (3) that you couldn't be baptized until you'd made that decision; and (4) that it was your duty as a Christian to spread that message.

There was no Baptist church in Palmerdale during my child-hood, so the family went to the big white church in the nearby town of Pinson three times a week—the Sunday morning and evening services and the Wednesday night prayer meeting. Only illness or the need to take care of Alice could keep us away.

I was fascinated by church. I couldn't get enough of the preach-ing. When I was five, our pastor told Dad he was impressed by my attentiveness. And I loved the daily Bible reading that was a regular part of our family's routine. My father would call down the hall of our home each evening and ask, "Son, have you read your Bible yet?" If I hadn't, I would answer, "No sir, not yet." Then I would slip quietly out of my small bed so as not to wake my two younger brothers, who slept in a bed next to mine, sit on the floor under the hall light, and study the daily reading.

In typical Baptist fashion, our pastor ended each Sunday morning service with an invitation to accept Christ or rededicate one's life. At a Sunday morning service when I was seven and looking after my little brother David, I felt moved to talk to the preacher when the invitation was given. I told David to stay in the pew and walked up to the front of the church. "I want to give my heart to Christ," I told the pastor. Soon after, I was baptized in the frigid water of nearby Turkey Creek.

A couple of years later, that church building was destroyed by fire despite the efforts of Dad, myself, and many others to save it. Fortunately, a new brick church soon rose on that site.

Soon thereafter the Baptists of Palmerdale formed their own congregation, meeting initially in a small wooden building on the edge of town. During the years of World War II, despite shortages and rationing, the congregation built with their own hands a large brick sanctuary that serves the Palmerdale Baptist Church to this day.

All of the Walkers were active in the church. Both Dad and Mother taught Sunday School and sang in the choir, and Dad served as Sunday school superintendent and was elected to the board of deacons, responsible for general maintenance and the material needs of the church. My siblings and I sang in the youth choir and were active in Sunday school and the Sunday evening Training Union, a program designed to help members learn to share their faith with others. During those years I was learning that faith should be expressed by serious, dependable work within the church.

As I grew, my spiritual life deepened because of my constant exposure to the Bible, preaching, and religious studies. After hearing a sermon on tithing, I decided I should tithe the dollar I made for doing some unusual chores. The first week, I placed a dime in the offering plate. The next Sunday I placed another dime, and the third Sunday another dime. Finally Dad became aware of what I was doing and explained that one dime would have been sufficient.

One day when I was eight, I took a break from reading my Bible and went for a walk in a field covered with sage next to the family home. Next to the woods, I found a large square rock surrounded by pine trees. That rock looked like an altar, and it reminded me of the Israelites bringing their offerings to the tabernacle. But what could I offer? I was wearing a toy holster, a Christmas present from my folks. I was a Lone Ranger fan, so Dad made me six silver wooden bullets to put in the belt of the holster. I loved those bullets, but I took them out and put them on that altar. For me that was a symbol of what my life would be like. God was telling me, "You're going to have to give up the things you think are most precious."

At the age of ten I felt a call to enter the ministry but said little about it at the time because of my youth and my uncertainty about the validity of the call. But as I grew older and entered Christian ministry, I had many occasions to remember the lesson of the silver bullets: Following the will of God often requires us to give up good things in order to pursue the very best goals, to pursue the true will of God.

MY FORMAL SCHOOLING BEGAN at the Palmerdale elementary school, a big new brick building with steam heat and a huge water tower. I was a good student when I tried, but I was a lot more interested in playing in the schoolyard than I was in studying. I was content with Bs and the occasional A.

Finding the right high school for me proved to be a challenge. I began high school in Pinson, but the students there were a rough group, and there was a lot of bullying. So in mid-year my parents transferred me to Phillips High School in Birmingham, my mother's alma mater. But there were also problems at Phillips. It was a large school with over two thousand students, intimidating for a boy from Palmerdale with its total population of five hundred. The students included veterans of World War II, tough guys who were much older than their classmates. I wanted to be on the football team, but I just couldn't compete with them. And coming up with bus fare to and from Birmingham was a stretch for the family budget. So for tenth grade I transferred yet again, this time to Jefferson County High School, eighteen miles away in Tarrant City.

Jefferson County High was about a quarter the size of Phillips, and I flourished there. I made the football team, but there were veterans at Jefferson County High, too, and I ended up as a sort of practice dummy. Still I persevered until I injured my wrist and decided it was time to leave the team. I made a lot of friends at that school and saw an opportunity to improve a number of things there. When I came to Jefferson County High, there was no student government and little sense of camaraderie or school spirit among the students, who were bused in from all over the county. So during my junior year, some of my classmates and I decided the school needed a student government. The principal agreed it was a good idea. I found myself making announcements at the school's monthly assemblies and got used to public speaking. As I was heading into my senior year, I decided to run for student body president.

In that election I was running against two or three other guys, and one of them was the quarterback of the football team. He was a good guy, and I fully expected him to win. My dad saw that I was a little discouraged and said, "Son, just do your best. Get in there and do your best." So I thought, *I'm going to give him a hard run.*

I got permission to put up signs and posted them everywhere in the school. On election day I was resigned to defeat and was shocked when I won by a landslide. And I made the most of that opportunity. Because I had decided to give up football, I could devote most of my time to this new office, and the students responded with a dramatic increase in school spirit.

The vice president of the student body was a Methodist preacher's son, so he and I were good buddies. We had lots of ideas to improve the school. The principal was a veteran and a tough guy; he shot down most of our ideas, and we were getting frustrated. Then my dad said, "Just keep throwing out ideas. If you give him enough, he'll have to approve some of them." So we bombarded him with so many ideas he had to say yes to a few. We put in ideas we thought would please him: a "Howdy Week" to develop some fellowship among the students and a cleanup day to clear the candy wrappers and other trash out of the hallways and schoolyard. He started to get behind us.

I even persuaded him to have a Religious Emphasis Day. I asked the vice president to give a devotional, and I got up and gave a little sermon. I preached for about ten minutes. Of course, any chance I could get to preach, I would. It was a typical Baptist sermon—"You'd better repent or you are going to hell," although I wasn't quite that blunt. The sermon was well received, but that was not my first experience as a preacher.

Summer was revival time in the Bible Belt, as the South is often called. Churches and tents would fill up with folks looking to have their faith renewed and their loved ones saved, or just wanting a night out. When I was fifteen, I asked the Palmerdale Baptist Church's pastor and deacons to let a youth group hold a youth revival at the church. The revival preachers were to be two of my cousins who were ministerial students at Howard College in Birmingham. I persuaded the pastor and all the deacons but one. The only deacon to vote against it was my dad. I was shocked. Dad was afraid I would be hurt if the revival wasn't a success. Thanks be to God, he needn't have worried.

The revival was drawing both young people and grownups. But no one was available to preach the climactic Sunday night service. I would have to preach.

As I was troubled by the lukewarm faith I found in many regular churchgoers, I decided to take Acts 26:27–28 as my text: "'King Agrippa, do you believe the prophets? I know that you do believe.' Then Agrippa said to Paul, 'You almost persuade me to become a Christian.'" What happened that night amazed me.

I preached with all the zeal I could because it was a burden on my heart. I said, "Some of you have been coming to these meetings, and you're almost persuaded to become a Christian, but you know in your heart you're not. You haven't given your heart to Christ." And that was all, the only thing I knew to preach: "Give your heart to Christ." At the climax of that sermon I invited people to gather at the front of the sanctuary to dedicate or rededicate themselves to Christ. Most of the congregation came forward. Young people and adults alike knelt on the floor to pray, pouring out their hearts to God.

They went back to their seats, and to my amazement, there were little puddles of tears all over the floor. Almost every place there'd been somebody kneeling, there were tears.

The effects of that night lasted two or three years and confirmed for me my calling to the ministry.

NEWS OF THE REVIVAL spread through the churches in the area. One young woman's father had started a prison ministry, and he'd been having a hard time finding preachers for it. His daughter suggested he ask me. So for three years I preached and witnessed in prisons. The prison ministry fired my determination to win souls for Christ, and it gave me something else: the knowledge that the Spirit is stronger than fear. One day my companions and I visited the large prison outside Montgomery, the state capital. The guards asked us if we wanted to visit the tuberculosis ward there and its dying, desperate prisoners. The group said yes.

In the TB ward I walked up to a prisoner and asked him, "Have you ever been saved?" Somehow, the man had smuggled in a switchblade knife, which he kept opening and closing, as if to say, "I can kill you any minute."

"I am not . . . never!" the man answered.

Despite the cold, threatening look in the man's eyes, I went on talking. Even if the only response I got was the opening and closing of the knife, I would do what God wanted.

THERE WAS MORE GOING ON in those teenage years than high school and learning something about preaching. For one thing, there was Mary Sue Henderson.

It seemed I had known Mary Sue all my life. When I was six, I went to children's Bible classes taught by Alma Henderson, whose family had moved into the house our family left when we moved into larger quarters. I loved the classes, and I loved Mrs. Henderson. I loved the hand-colored pictures she put up on the felt board, and I loved learning Bible stories about Jacob and the other characters in the Old Testament. The class was held right across the street from the Palmerdale school, and I would drop in when I didn't need to go straight home to help my mother with Alice. Also in the Bible class, sitting on the floor with the other children, was Mrs. Henderson's daughter, Mary Sue, a year younger than I. The next year, both of us were at the Palmerdale school; I was in the second grade and Mary Sue in the first.

The Hendersons belonged to the Christian and Missionary Alliance (CMA), but when they couldn't get to Eastlake in Birmingham, where the nearest CMA church was located, they'd walk the half-mile to our Baptist church. When I began to be interested in girls, I went on a date or two, but I thought most of the girls I knew were less than fully committed Christians. Mary Sue Henderson was different. Not only did she sometimes attend Sunday morning services at the Baptist church, but she was a regular at the Sunday night services and the Wednesday night prayer meeting. And in addition to all that, she was beautiful and fun to be with. I learned later that Mary Sue thought I was the handsomest boy in town. We quickly became a couple, and neither of us was about to date anyone else—almost.

The Hendersons wanted their daughter to have a thoroughly Christian education, something they didn't think they'd be able to give her near home. So they enrolled her in the Bob Jones Academy in Greenville, South Carolina, 250 miles away. We wrote faithfully, and I once drove to South Carolina to visit. We dated happily every summer. But I was something of an iconoclast. I didn't care much for Valentine's Day, and on February 14, when Mary Sue checked her mailbox at Bob Jones, there was nothing there from me. Instead, she got a phone call from one of her friends telling her I had taken another girl to the church's Sweetheart Banquet.

"I was ticked off," Mary Sue remembers. "He had no idea what going steady meant—that you didn't go out with anyone else." When I found out how upset she was, I called to explain that I'd been pressured into it by some people at church, only to be told our relationship was off. It wasn't until Mary Sue was back in Palmerdale after graduating high school and I was commuting to college that we got back together. The way Mary Sue tells it:

"I was working in the bank, and my aqua party dress was at the cleaners. Gordon asked me to go with him to a church social. It was a kind of last-minute thing, but since I'd had my dress cleaned and the cleaner was close to the bank, I said yes. So we got back together again because of an aqua dress."

We were a couple again, and this time it was for good.

MANY PEOPLE IN MY HOME COMMUNITY had long believed I had all the gifts I needed to be a successful preacher and pastor. The dreams of flying over that cattle ranch in Texas were gone. I enjoyed preaching and witnessing. But it was still a struggle for me to accept the path God had chosen for me. I hadn't had a Damascus road experience, a sudden and overwhelming call. I knew it had to be God's choice, not mine. I prayed earnestly and longed to know the way He wanted me to go. In the end, I was sure of where the Holy Spirit was leading me. And it became increasingly clear that I would share that path with Mary Sue, the love of my life.

Gordon preaching, September 1971

CHAPTER 2

Preacher Boy

WHEN I WENT AWAY TO COLLEGE in the fall of 1949, I
didn't have far to go. The East Lake campus of Howard College was only fifteen miles from Palmerdale. Founded in
1841 by the Alabama Baptist Convention, Howard offered me
more than a college education; it gave me a chance to widen my
outreach, grow as a preacher and teacher, and learn how to be
a pastor.

Today Howard College has grown to become Samford University, with nearly five thousand students, half of them under-
graduates, enjoying a 180-acre campus. But in 1949 it was just
four square blocks with five hundred students. It was an easy
commute from Palmerdale, so during my freshman and sophomore years I lived at home and continued to help my father in the
grocery store.

I had no doubts as to why I was at Howard: to prepare myself
for seminary and eventual ordination as a pastor. I majored in
religion, taking Bible classes, church history, and theology. And
there were other learning opportunities for prospective ministers.

The summer after my freshman year, I was asked to preach at a revival in a church near Dothan in southern Alabama. Almost all the church members came, and they were joined by people from churches in the surrounding communities. The results were the same as those at the Palmerdale youth revival: many came forward and knelt as I urged them to give their hearts to Christ. Before the summer was over, I was invited to preach at other revivals in the area. One of the churches where I preached asked me to be their pastor, and soon other churches were asking as well.

The little country churches I served were poor; they couldn't afford to support a full-time pastor, and even a part-time pastor, a "preacher boy" college student, strained their resources. One of the churches that wanted me to be their pastor could only afford me for one Sunday a month—quarter time, it's called. I was coming down to one of the other churches every other Sunday, so I told them, "Since I'm already coming down here two Sundays a month, I'll preach for you on the two other Sundays if you'll just pay for my gasoline." They agreed to that. Gas for the four-hundred-mile round trip cost me around fifty dollars a month. That little church always had a minimum of thirty dollars a month to pay me, and with the thirty-five dollars from the other church, I had about five dollars a week left after paying my expenses. I thought I was doing pretty well.

The members of my new congregations were farmers. Even though we had only four and a half acres to farm in Palmerdale, I felt like I was one of them. And I visited them. Their other pastors had been farmers or held down other jobs and hadn't had time for visiting. I made up my mind to stop by at every home in the area served by each of my two churches, staying to chat or share a meal. The people loved me, and I loved them.

My confidence in my vocation was growing, and during the Christmas break in my sophomore year, I asked Mary Sue to marry me. It was to be a long engagement; we planned to marry after I finished college. On one of my preaching trips to southern Alabama, I found a ring at a jewelry store in Dothan. When I showed it to my mother, she couldn't believe it. It wasn't that big a ring, but it looked awfully big to my mother; it was bigger than hers. She said, "Son, how are you going to pay for this?"

I said, "Just a little bit at a time, Mother," and that's how I paid for it, twenty-five dollars a month.

AS MY PASTORAL RESPONSIBILITIES GREW, I moved onto the Howard campus, returning to Palmerdale once or twice a week to help Dad at the grocery store. I did the heavy lifting, moving sacks of seed and fertilizer and bales of hay, and earned a few extra dollars to help with expenses. Then, at the end of my sophomore year at Howard, a preacher-boy friend asked me to preach at Mt. Hebron Baptist Church in Leeds, not far from the college. Founded in 1817 to serve the ex-soldiers from Andrew Jackson's army who had settled the area, the church seated two hundred, but the congregation had dwindled to twenty-five, and the church was in danger of closing. In a last attempt to save it, the deacons were looking for a new pastor, and after hearing me preach, they offered me the job. Sensing their desperation, I felt I had to accept. I would move into the little house next to the church and commute to school from there.

Now that I had a home for us, Mary Sue and I decided to move up our wedding date. It wasn't easy. The first time I went to get the wedding license, I was turned away. I was only twenty, and in

Alabama, a man had to be twenty-one to get married without his father's permission. The next time I brought my father—but not the bride. I had to persuade the clerk to let me sign the license for her. To this day Mary Sue jokingly wonders if we are legally married.

The wedding was on June 5, 1952, and we began our married life in the pastor's house next to the Leeds church. The house was less than ideal. It had six rooms but no bathroom. The only plumbing was a spigot of cold water in the kitchen. The parishioners were proud of that. You didn't have to go out and pump water from the well.

Visits to the outhouse could be eventful. One day Mary Sue was on her way there when a little black snake crossed her path. I was in the house when I heard her bloodcurdling scream. "Honey, it's only a little black snake," I said, trying to reassure her. "I don't care; it's a snake!" she said.

Just after we moved into our house I organized the summer revival at the church. Like the other revivals I had preached, this one was a success, thanks be to God. I baptized more than thirty people, most of them adults, with six teenagers.

These were young men, tough guys. They weren't nice little country boys. Some of them had fought in the war; they'd seen a lot and done a lot. So it was really marvelous to have this baptism. There was a beautiful creek not far from the church, wide and deep, where we baptized them. The first to be baptized was Mary Sue. She had been baptized in the Christian and Missionary Alliance, but the Baptists recognized only their own baptisms. This was among the first of many concessions Mary Sue willingly made on my behalf. I'm so thankful for her.

I started a Bible class for these new converts. My teaching, carefully explaining the Scriptures verse by verse, and the visits I paid to the people in what was called the "church field" began to grow the church, till soon more than a hundred were attending.

With new people came new tensions: the old guard resented the newcomers I was bringing in, while the new members were impatient with the stubbornness of the old guard. As the pressure grew, the congregation threatened to split.

Although I had graduated from Howard in 1953 and was ready to go to seminary, I stayed in Leeds for an extra six months to help a new church, Valley View Baptist, get started. This was my fourth pastorate, but the first church I had helped to start. Even at that early date I felt believers should follow the example of the New Testament church, although I did not know exactly what that meant. I had no idea how powerful that conviction would become in future years or how it would change my life. The people at Valley View were optimistic and dedicated, and the church grew rapidly, even as Mt. Hebron continued to grow as well.

My first choice for seminary was Southwestern Baptist Theological Seminary in Fort Worth, Texas. I bought an old trailer, loaded it up, and drove to Fort Worth to look the place over. Although I liked what I saw, I couldn't quite make up my mind to stay there. Something wouldn't let me do it. Darrell Hall, who introduced me to the folks at Mt. Hebron, wanted to help me find a church to pastor near the seminary, and he had me preach the Sunday we were there. I said to him, "Darrell, I just don't feel I can stay here. There's a new Baptist seminary in Berkeley, California, and I think maybe God's calling me to go there." He understood the call of God and told me to do what I needed to do.

That winter, Mary Sue pregnant with our first child, we loaded up our trailer, and with two hundred dollars travel money, we headed out west for the spring semester at Golden Gate Baptist Theological Seminary. On Christmas Eve we arrived at my uncle's house in Sacramento, where we stayed until it was time to register at the seminary.

It was a hard time. We were lonesome and aching to be back in Alabama. But we found an apartment in Berkeley, and I enrolled in school. It was a tiring grind, pumping gas in the evenings after a full day of classes to keep us going. I wondered why on earth we had come. If God had called us to Berkeley, I thought, it was to help prepare us to face tribulation.

That summer I served as an interim pastor for three months at a church in nearby San Jose. When the regular pastor returned, we went back home so that I could help Dad at the grocery store. On Wednesday nights and Sundays, Mary Sue and I went out to Leeds so that I could preach at Mt. Hebron.

But when it was time to go back to California for the next semester, the people in Leeds asked me to stay with them for a year to pastor at Valley View. Dad and I went out to Berkeley, hitched up the old trailer, and headed back to Alabama.

By the time we got to Los Angeles, Dad wasn't feeling well. He was having chest pains and was worried that it was his heart. Dad said, "Now son, if I die, I don't want you stopping anywhere; take me home to Alabama." I told him I wasn't going to drive across the country with a corpse in the car. I pushed that little car to haul that trailer back home as fast as it could go. It turned out to be a false alarm, and after some rest, Dad was even able to do a little of the driving.

THE NEXT YEAR IN LEEDS WAS FRUITFUL, although difficult, alternating between the Mt. Hebron and Valley View factions. But it had its rewards. It was good to see the new church growing. And it was even better to see our family grow, when Mary Sue gave birth to our first child, a daughter. We named her Deborah Sue.

During the dead of winter that year (1953–54), Darrell Hall and I went on a three-month mission trip to Berlin, Germany, to share the love of Christ with the poor residents of that beleaguered city. Despite the bitter cold and the language barrier, we felt our message was well received and produced a number of converts. The experience only whetted my desire to pursue a career in missions.

When the year was up and it was time to go back to seminary, I was more than ready to try Southwestern. The job prospects in Fort Worth seemed bleak; the seminary students fanned out all over the countryside looking for opportunities to preach. But my friend Darrell Hall was looking out for me again. Darrell steered me to a little church in Crowley, Texas, a few miles from the seminary, and I went out to preach there before the semester began. They immediately asked me to be their pastor. It wasn't an easy job. The search committee told me the congregation was split right down the middle. I carefully picked my way through the factional fighting and pastored the church for three and a half years.

Despite the difficulties, we spent fruitful years in Fort Worth. I enjoyed working with the congregation, and I loved that prairie country. And I was learning. Southwestern Seminary dwarfed Howard College, with two thousand students on a campus dominated by the chapel's golden dome, visible from our front yard.

As always, I loved studying the Bible. I took to the conservative Baptist theology that prevailed at Southwestern. My church history course introduced me to Athanasius, Ignatius, and the other fathers of the first Christian centuries, but at this point they were only names. The first Christians, I thought, must have been "Baptists in togas."

I appreciated my professors, both in the classroom and in informal conversations. One of the professors I most respected was C. E. Autrey, who taught the evangelism courses and went on to become director of evangelism for the Southern Baptist Convention. If I could find any time at all to talk to him, I'd take it. If I could find any reason, I'd go in and ask him questions, because I loved talking to him.

From the beginning of my road to ministry, I had longed to go to the mission field, to Africa, to take the gospel where it was most needed. Mary Sue wanted to go with me. So she began to take courses to prepare her for certification by the Southern Baptist Mission Board. But it was not to be.

EMPHASIZING THAT AN ESPECIALLY VIRULENT strain of polio was headed our way from southwest Texas, the seminary physician strongly advised all students to have their children vaccinated against polio. We were uncertain about doing that, because for months Debbie had suffered one illness after another—sore throats, fevers, ear aches. But the doctor insisted, so four-year-old Debbie began a three-shot course of the Salk killed-virus vaccine. Unfortunately, the effects of the vaccine were different from what we expected.

Shortly after the second shot, she became ill with symptoms

of polio, as the epidemic spread through the community. Her condition rapidly deteriorated, and it soon became obvious that she had the dreaded bulbar form of polio—the type in which the respiratory muscles become paralyzed— from which many victims do not recover.

Within days Debbie required breathing help from the iron lung. Because other victims at the hospital (and nationwide) required this support for many months—and some permanently—Mary Sue and I feared the worst, but we prayed for the best possible outcome.

About four weeks after the onset, Deborah was removed from the iron lung briefly for cleaning purposes. The nurses noted how well she breathed, and Debbie did not want to go back into the big tank. Several days later she was removed for what was expected to be a brief interval, and one of the doctors saw how well she was breathing. He prescribed a trial without the iron lung, and she never required that device again.

At some point during her hospitalization, the doctors apologetically informed us that the vaccination might well have transmitted polio to Debbie. In those early days of killed-virus vaccination, sometimes the virus was not totally inactivated and could still cause the disease, a problem that has since been eliminated. Such were the vagaries of polio vaccination in that era.

Six weeks after entering the hospital, Debbie returned home to begin a year of physical therapy. Polio had left her with a paralyzed left arm but with some use of her left hand. Her other weakened muscles all returned to normal, thanks in large part to the intense physical therapy regimen Mary Sue administered after giving up her academic classes.

Debbie's recovery, especially in such a brief interval, seemed miraculous. But the real miracle is how Debbie dealt with her "handicap" in the years to follow. She performed well academically and as an adult worked for the county social services department. She sings in the church choir, drives a car, and has participated in all sorts of other activities. She and her husband Michael even adopted two children.

YET EVEN IF THE WAY TO AFRICA was closed to us because of Debbie's health, I hadn't lost my radical vision: to spread the gospel throughout the world in this generation. In a few years, I would have the opportunity to live it out. For now, however, God would find us a mission field closer to home.

I learned that the seminary had maps showing where there were Southern Baptist churches, including those searching for a pastor, but there was no effective means to match graduates with prospective churches. A friend and I worked out a system to help with that match. As a result of using that system, Mary Sue and I were called to a small mission church in the city of Xenia, Ohio—a different mission field from the one we originally had in mind, but nonetheless a true mission opportunity.

CHAPTER 3

The Crash

THE CITY OF XENIA, OHIO, twenty-one miles from Dayton in the southwestern part of the state, had about twenty thousand inhabitants when we moved there in 1960. Very few of them were Southern Baptists. Dayton Avenue Baptist Church was a struggling mission congregation of fifty. Although I was only twenty-eight and had only recently graduated from seminary, I already had a lot of experience as a pastor.

The members of the congregation were working-class people, many employed at the auto factories in Dayton. They were excited to be getting a new pastor and rented a house for us in a large development of two- and three-bedroom houses. It was nothing fancy, but it was a comfortable house, with small front and back yards, nicer than the houses we had lived in before.

I did the same things in Ohio that had worked for me in Alabama and Texas: Bible preaching and teaching, home visits, and revival meetings. It wasn't long before the congregation had doubled.

Our years in Xenia were a blessing. I was enthusiastic about the work, but I had a sense that something was missing. I wasn't quite sure what it was, but preaching through the Book of Acts, I wondered about our connection to the ancient church. Despite my questions, I tried to do my best.

Soon our little mission was not so little. It had outgrown the space we were renting in a school building. A generous man who owned property not far from our home offered to make available three acres on which to build a church. He wanted to encourage us, and he let us have the land at a very low price, well below market value. We knew God was providing for us in a supernatural way. Within three years, the congregation had put up two buildings on the property.

Despite our love for our work in Xenia, Africa was still on our minds. Mary Sue planned to complete her coursework and be certified by the Southern Baptist Foreign Mission Board. Then we'd go to bring the gospel to one of the places that needed it most. But again, God had other plans.

I WAS IN HIGH SPIRITS as I walked to the little four-seater. I'd always wanted to fly a plane, and I was thinking about getting a pilot's license. Today I'd get a chance for some practical experience at the plane's controls.

When I told Mary Sue about the flight, she begged me not to go. "It'll be fine, honey," I told her. "The deacon's son is flying the plane. He has plenty of experience; he flew in World War II. I'll be perfectly safe." But she was still uneasy.

There were three people walking to the plane with me: an old friend from Southwestern Seminary (who was helping out with a revival we were holding at our church that week), the plane's pilot, and the pilot's wife. The pilot had come from Nashville to lead the music during the revival, and he'd promised me a chance to take the controls.

When we got into the plane, I took the seat next to the pilot. The pilot's wife sat behind her husband, and my evangelist friend sat behind me. We buckled our seatbelts, and our pilot began going through his pre-flight checklist.

The little plane taxied to the middle of the runway. The pilot had never needed much of a run-up for takeoff. But today he was carrying more weight than he was used to: three passengers.

The airport manager later told me she'd looked up from her work to watch the takeoff. She was horrified: Our plane seemed to be heading straight for the fence. She breathed a sigh of relief as she saw it barely make it over. Silently I thanked the Lord for giving us a boost.

We flew northeast to Springfield, Ohio, where the pilot showed me how to land the plane. When we circled around Dayton, I got my chance to handle the controls. Apart from the scare at takeoff, the flight was just what I had wanted.

As we turned back to the airport to make our landing approach, the pilot seemed worried. "I don't have a lot of room at this airport to make a mistake," he said. And then he made one.

When he cut the throttle to slow down for the landing, a buzzer began to sound—the plane had stalled. Then he made another mistake. He pulled on the throttle to rev up the engine and then cut it a second time. The buzzer went off again. Thirty-five feet from the ground, the plane nosed over and headed straight down. I was sure we were going to die.

But after the plane hit the ground, I was still alive. I wasn't even unconscious. It felt like I was super-conscious. My mind was focused on everything that was happening around me.

I could see that we were all still in danger; we had to get out before the plane caught fire.

The door on the pilot's side was jammed shut; only the door on my side would open. I pulled myself out. I had no feeling in my feet, but I didn't have time to think about that. All I could think of was getting the others out of the plane.

A friend of mine, the pastor of a Nazarene church who was also a pilot, was at the airport gassing up his plane. When our plane went down, he ran to his car and rushed over to where we were. Smoke was curling up from the wreckage. When the pastor got there, I was helping everybody out of the plane and telling them to get away.

When I knew the three others were safe, I asked the pastor to drive me to my doctor's office. I was bleeding pretty heavily; my face had slammed against the control panel and the bones in my nose and face were broken.

When we got to the doctor's office, he took one look and sent me to the hospital. By the time I got to the emergency room, I was covered with blood. I couldn't feel anything below my knees. Many years later I learned that the injury my legs suffered on impact led to the painful peripheral neuropathy I developed a few years later, which grew worse with each year.

I was in the hospital for eight days. While I lay in my bed, my mind was full of questions: *What does all this mean? Why did I survive what I thought was sudden death? What is God trying to tell me?*

God uses even our darkest moments to bring us closer to Him. The crash taught me two things: Life is so short that we've got to make every minute count, and to do that I had to know what

God wanted me to do. I prayed hard, asking the Lord to show me the way. Mary Sue often comments that the Lord wanted me to learn a third thing as well: I should listen more to the wife He gave me! I'm sure she has a point there.

The answer to my prayers seemed clear. We'd had success in Xenia, and we loved the people at our church, but it was time to move on. But where would I go, and what would I do? We couldn't go to Africa; once again, Mary Sue had put her coursework aside, this time to care for me. She wouldn't qualify to be a Southern Baptist missionary.

As a result of the work we had done in Xenia and my love of evangelism, I'd been asked to be chairman of evangelism for the Greater Dayton Baptist Association. I was happy to have been given the responsibility, and as part of that work, I invited Gene Edwards, another friend of mine from Southwestern and an accomplished church planter, to speak to the pastors of the Dayton area Baptist churches.

During his visit, Gene stayed with us, and I had an opportunity to talk to him about the vision for evangelization I'd developed when I was in seminary.

"You know," I said, "for many years my hope has been the evangelization of the world in our generation."

Gene thought for a moment. "That's how Bill Bright signs all his letters," he said. "You need to meet Bill Bright."

"Who's Bill Bright?" I asked.

"He's the president of Campus Crusade for Christ."

"What's that?"

"It's a great ministry working with college kids all over the country," Gene explained.

"But I'm hoping to go to Africa as a missionary," I said. "Why do I need to check out Campus Crusade?"

"I think you'd make a great campus evangelist," Gene answered. "I can call a friend of mine in the Chicago area who's the Big Ten Regional Director for Campus Crusade. Since you're here in Ohio, why don't we get him on the phone and let him tell you what Campus Crusade is? Then the two of you can set up a meeting."

I felt as if I were in a whirlwind. Fifteen minutes earlier I'd known nothing about Campus Crusade, and now Gene was urging me to join it.

Gene reached for the phone. "I want you to talk to Peter Gillquist," he said.

CHAPTER 4

Campus Crusade

THE VOICE AT THE OTHER END of the phone was deep and bubbling with good spirits. I liked Peter Gillquist at once. After we'd introduced ourselves and chatted a little, Peter invited me to meet him in Columbus, Ohio, the home of Ohio State University.

Peter Gillquist was twenty-five when I met him. At thirty-two, I was his elder by seven years. Peter had gone to the University of Minnesota, where one Monday night in Lent, a Campus Crusade team visited his fraternity, Sigma Alpha Epsilon (SAE). Something in their message appealed to him, and he soon began talking with Ray Nethery, the Campus Crusade leader at Minnesota. A few weeks later, he made his commitment to Christ. After stints at Dallas Theological Seminary and Wheaton Graduate School, Peter became a full-time worker for Campus Crusade.

Campus Crusade for Christ was one of the largest and most successful organizations to come out of the post–World War II evangelical revival. Founded in 1951 by a Fuller Seminary student named Bill Bright, by 1963 it had chapters at colleges and universities all over the country. Campus Crusade energetically evangelized students, not satisfied to simply wait for them to come to its meetings as did many campus-based denominational ministries. The organization was staffed by people from a variety of denominations, brought together by their love of Christ and the gospel message. They conducted Bible studies, get-togethers, and discussion groups, but as a parachurch movement, it evangelized students but didn't compete with the evangelical churches. It left baptism and the Lord's Supper to them.

Peter was in Belmont, Illinois, 285 miles away. It was winter, and with all the ice and snow he didn't want to drive or fly to Columbus. He took the train, and I drove the 53 miles from Xenia to Columbus and met him at the station. From there we drove straight to the Ohio State campus. Ohio State had 25,000 students, one of the largest student bodies in the country. For a preacher boy from Palmerdale, it was overwhelming.

Peter headed us toward Fraternity Row. I felt uneasy; I'd been brought up to think frat houses were dens of iniquity.

Peter knocked on the door of the SAE house. "Hi, I'm Peter Gillquist," he said. "I'm an SAE brother from the University of Minnesota, and I'd like to meet your chapter president."

When the president came downstairs, Peter introduced himself and began witnessing to him. They talked for about fifteen minutes, until it was time for the president to go to class. He seemed to have been impressed by the conversation. "If you'd like to talk to the vice president," he told Peter, "I'll bring him down."

Peter's confidence was amazing. I was bowled over by how simply and easily he talked about Christ and kept the fraternity men listening. *I'd like to be able to do that*, I thought. *If I could be a half, or even just a third as good as he is, I'd be satisfied.* We knocked on a few more doors on Fraternity Row and then walked around the campus while Peter talked to me about Campus Crusade.

As I headed back home after dropping Peter off at the train station, conflicting thoughts were running through my head. On the one hand, I'd been so impressed by Peter and the work he was doing. That kind of work would be a challenge for me, and I've always liked challenges. On the other hand, I was the pastor of a flourishing church, and it would be hard to leave— especially for something I wasn't sure I could do in the first place. *I'd need a call from God to join Campus Crusade*, I thought.

When I got home, I talked things over with Mary Sue. "Oh, that sounds interesting," she said noncommittally. She shared my uncertainty. Would Campus Crusade be a good fit for us? Would my age make it harder for me to establish rapport with the students? We prayed fervently that God would show us what to do.

We were surprised when Peter invited us to come out to California for Campus Crusade's summer staff training sessions. Crusade had recently bought a large old hotel in Arrowhead Springs, in the mountains just outside of San Bernardino, and made it their new headquarters. That summer they would be having their staff conference there for the first time.

At the Los Angeles airport we were met by two Crusade staffers: the secretary from the office, and the Women's National Field Coordinator, Dianne Ross. Like Peter, they talked about Christ simply and naturally. They filled me in on what was going on in Campus Crusade. I was impressed by what they had to say; the dynamism of the organization and the scope of its work appealed to the evangelist in me. *I'd like to be a part of this*, I thought. *But how can I make it happen?*

The first class I attended was taught by Jon Braun, the men's national field coordinator for Crusade and the best speaker in the organization. He was dazzling. He lifted the dynamism and decibels to a whole new level. I couldn't keep from listening to him. Billy Graham had been my model as a preacher, but Jon was even more impressive. All the people I'd met so far at Crusade, Peter and Dianne and Jon, were special. Crusade was drawing me in.

Our two weeks at Arrowhead Springs constituted a life-changing experience for Mary Sue and me. The organization's ministry and vision attracted me and challenged me to grow in my own ministry. And when we met Bill Bright and heard him speak, we found his message just as challenging. He spoke on the evangelization of the world in this generation, which had been my hope since seminary.

Bill then took up the theme of thanksgiving, taking as his text 1 Thessalonians 5:16–18: "Rejoice always, pray without ceasing, in everything give thanks; for this is the will of God in Christ Jesus for you." Then he asked us to go to our rooms and make a list of all the things for which we had never given thanks. That night we got down on our knees and thanked God for things we'd never even thought of giving thanks for: Debbie's polio, my sister's handicaps, our struggles in California, the difficulties I'd had making it through seminary—all the troubles we'd lived through.

When the conference was over, I agreed to join the Campus Crusade staff and start working at Ohio State in the fall. It wasn't easy to leave our Dayton Avenue church; Mary Sue and I loved the people there, and we could feel their love for us. I learned a lot there about pastoring and growing a church. The congregation hadn't yet completed its new buildings, but I was confident they could finish without any problems, because I knew the Holy Spirit was calling me to Campus Crusade.

There was still one big problem: Campus Crusade would pay me $450 a month—less than the Xenia church was paying me—but my salary wouldn't start until the fall. The three months I'd spend training during the summer would be unpaid. We had no savings and no way to earn the money.

My friend Gene Edwards, who introduced me to Peter Gillquist, happened to be in Xenia to lead a conference. At one of the meetings he said, "I want you all to know that Gordon Walker and his wife are going to leave to go to Campus Crusade for Christ. That means they're resigning their church and their support, and they need four hundred and fifty dollars a month to pay their salary.

"I want you to bow your heads and close your eyes. I've got some cards here, and if you feel God is putting it into your heart to pledge ten dollars a month for the next three months, I want you to sign those cards and then raise your hand."

He paused for a few minutes and looked up to count the raised hands. Then he started laughing. "I knew this would happen," he said. "I only gave out forty-five cards, and forty-five of you have raised your hands." We had the money we needed. I now had no doubt that I was going where God wanted me to go.

I still keep those cards in my desk drawer.

I spent time with Peter Gillquist in Chicago to learn the ropes. Then Mary Sue and I went back out to Arrowhead Springs. I was surprised to find that, even though I was a newcomer, I had been assigned as a teacher in Crusade's Institute of Bible Studies. I taught my favorite subject: Paul's letter to the Romans.

That fall, we moved into a duplex house on the OSU campus. At thirty-five I was the oldest member of the Campus Crusade staff, but I was determined not to be the least energetic. Every Sunday night we had meetings at our house to fellowship and teach young Christians and to share our message with the curious. As always, Mary Sue offered our guests a seemingly limitless hospitality. Eventually, we made space so that young people who needed some guidance or just a temporary place to stay could live with us.

We weren't only concerned with the students' spiritual needs; we wanted to do all we could to give their lives direction and help them to have a happy future. Sometimes that went beyond advice to a little matchmaking. One of the students staying at our house was a girl from Mississippi who had been a beauty queen. She had suffered an accident, and one of her legs was in a cast. One day as I was walking across the campus, I spotted a young Lutheran pastor I knew. He was a fine young man, dedicated to Christ—and unmarried. "Why don't you come up to our house?" I asked. "There's a young lady there I'd like you to meet."

When we got to the house, I took the young man upstairs to meet the former beauty queen from Mississippi. He liked her from day one. But she was angry at me. "Gordon," she said, "why did you do that to me? I didn't have a chance to put on any makeup!" Her lack of makeup certainly hadn't bothered my pastor friend, and their relationship grew and deepened. It was no surprise to Mary Sue and me when they decided to get married.

Herb McCollum (who later became Fr. Mark), a 1964 freshman, was one of my first—and best—student friends at OSU and has remained a strong friend since those days. Before he began his freshman year, his uncle, worried that Herb would be going to a non-Christian school, brought him to a men's retreat. It so happened that I was conducting the retreat. Herb's uncle made sure his nephew met me, and I made the young man promise to come and see me when he got to campus.

Herb and I literally bumped into one another during his freshman orientation. I invited him to the Campus Crusade meeting we were holding at nine that night at our house. Herb was hooked. He stayed in Campus Crusade throughout college, even becoming our OSU chapter president.

The 1960s weren't peaceful years on many American campuses. Faced with the Vietnam War, students rejected the morals of their parents, indulging their appetites for sex and drugs, pledging to "never trust anyone over thirty." Everything from peaceful demonstrations to the occupation of buildings and vandalism disrupted campuses from Berkeley to Columbus. Our campus was not immune.

I searched for ways to show the students that there were alternatives to the counterculture. Finally we devised Operation Other Side to show students the other side of the story—a week of activities designed to tell the whole campus about Christ.

Our logo was a stylized door opening, which echoed Revelation 3:20: "Behold, I stand at the door and knock. If anyone hears My voice and opens the door, I will come in to him and dine with him, and he with Me." I got Tom Barrington, a star football player and a leader in both Campus Crusade and the

Fellowship of Christian Athletes, to serve as our co-chairman. Crusade students gathered at the Oval at the center of the campus and handed out tracts. I gave out tracts myself and talked to any students who would listen. Given the atmosphere at OSU, those weren't easy things to do. We held Bible studies, coordinated by Herb McCollum, on Monday, Tuesday, and Wednesday nights at 175 locations. The week ended on Saturday night with a concert by Campus Crusade's New Folk Singers in the big OSU auditorium.

I was elated by the success of the week—Crusade even considered repeating it on other campuses—but it was exhausting. I remember sitting with Herb in the small office in our basement, too tired to get up and go upstairs to answer the phone.

During those years Campus Crusade was growing, and I was growing with it. Soon I was directing all of our work in Ohio. I expanded my horizons—and the scope of our evangelizing—by beginning an international student ministry. Then in 1966 Bill Bright asked me to take over Crusade's work in Africa. It was the fulfillment of my dream, but not in the way I'd imagined it. I made two long trips, visiting Ghana, Kenya, and Nigeria, meeting with college students who might become Crusade's African leaders. On my second trip, Mary Sue was able to join me for a month. We seriously considered moving to Africa, but because of Debbie's needs and our growing family, we decided against it.

I WAS GIVING A HUNDRED PERCENT of my energy to Campus Crusade, but at the same time I had misgivings about where that work was going. We were bringing students to Christ and studying the Bible with them, but we couldn't baptize them or celebrate the Lord's Supper. We were supposed to encourage them to join a local church; many of them never did.

I knew the Apostle Paul had said again and again that the church was the body of Christ; Campus Crusade, I thought, was an arm without a body. And I wasn't alone in thinking so. A group that included Peter Gillquist, my Campus Crusade mentor; Jon Braun, our star preacher; Jack Sparks, a Pennsylvania State PhD who had come to Campus Crusade to work with faculty members; Richard Ballew, an accomplished Bible teacher; Ray Nethery, who had discipled Peter Gillquist and was now a Campus Crusade vice president; Ken Berven, an assistant to Bill Bright; and other concerned staff members began meeting to discuss the situation.

We met in the afternoons at a department-store restaurant in San Bernardino to eat strawberry pie and talk theology. Church was the focus of our conversations. Campus Crusade insisted it wasn't a church, that it was serving the churches by making new Christians and not competing with them. But many of our converts never joined a church, were never baptized, and never received communion. Disciplined Christian living began where Campus Crusade stopped. The logical thing, we thought, was to bring church to Campus Crusade. Then we could baptize, celebrate the Lord's Supper, worship regularly, and have the fellowship of a regular congregation.

I went to Bill Bright to explain the problem. Bill reiterated that Crusade was a parachurch organization, an arm of the churches, not a church itself. Now, I had been a pastor; I knew how important the church was in living a Christian life. Bill's answer frustrated me. Paul's church was the Body of Christ, where all the different parts work together. What use is an arm without a body?

Meanwhile, the focus on the church at our afternoon meetings intensified. What was the church? we asked ourselves. What had it looked like in New Testament times? Where was it now? How could the Protestant churches, with their differing doctrines, be the church? Was one of these churches the one Christ had founded? And how did our work in Crusade fit into the picture?

Those of us who were worried about Crusade's limits met in early 1968 at Kansas State University in Manhattan, Kansas, to discuss the direction the organization should take. All of us reported directly to Bill Bright, and when Bill found out about the meeting, he was furious. We went directly to Arrowhead Springs, where eleven of us went to see him. "We have to work out what the church really is," we told him. Again, Bill was furious. He was particularly angry at me for attending the meeting. He'd had confidence in me, and he felt betrayed.

"Men," Bill said, "you're just going to have to do that on your own." We took that as an invitation to us to leave Crusade. Over the next few months Peter, Dick Ballew, Jack Sparks, Ray Nethery, Ken Berven, Jon Braun, and other staff members—the core leadership of Campus Crusade—resigned. Crusade was in turmoil.

For the moment, I stayed. I was committed to my African students and didn't want to suddenly abandon them. But the choice to stay was a tough one; the men who had left were my closest friends. I taught at the summer institute that year, but it wasn't the same.

When the institute was over, Bill sent a letter to the staff. "We had a wonderful summer," he wrote. "Now that those who were dissidents have left us, we can all speak with one voice." To me, this was another invitation to leave. But it wasn't yet the right time.

In addition to my work at OSU, I'd been teaching Bible classes in Mansfield, Ohio, about sixty miles northeast of Columbus. I felt it was time to begin detaching myself from campus work and give the new staff of Campus Crusade the freedom to work on their own. So our family moved from Columbus to a garage apartment in Mansfield—all six of us!

I had enrolled in the graduate program in philosophy at OSU, and I drove down from Mansfield on Tuesdays and Thursdays to attend classes. I spent all day in Columbus teaching Bible classes. In the morning I taught mostly women; then I'd go over to the campus and teach a noon class at the student union. Eventually we had sixty or seventy kids in the class. The dining commons in the student union was an open space, and I had to teach the class over the noise. In the evening we led a couples group at a local church.

Mary Sue and I started looking for a farmhouse in Mansfield to rent. We had a friend there, Harold "Hod" Bolesky. Hod was wealthy; his brother had invented a new kind of thermostat, and the family business, Therm-O-Disk, was prospering. Hod was a modest man and a committed Christian. He funded the local Christian school and provided scholarships for OSU students to attend Crusade's Summer Bible Institutes.

When I told Hod and his wife, Lillian, that we were looking for a house, they told me they had a farm that Hod dedicated to the Lord to be used for youth work, and they urged us to take a look at it. Hod and Lillian had named the place Grace Haven Farm.

Ray Nethery (left) and Gordon baptize a new Christian at Grace Haven Farm, 1971

CHAPTER 5

Grace Haven Farm

MARY SUE AND I FELL IN LOVE with Grace Haven Farm the first time we saw it. But the farmhouse already had tenants—the principal of the Christian school and his family. We wondered where on the farm we could live. We were overwhelmed when Hod and Lillian offered to build a new house on the farm especially for our family. I made a sketch of what we'd need: extra bedrooms for troubled youth who would stay with us, and a big basement to use for our retreats. Hod's brother-in-law, who was in the construction business, agreed to build it. In November 1968, I sent Bill Bright my formal resignation.

Within days after I resigned, we found ourselves in a new crisis. Work on the house was almost done, and Mary Sue and our three-year-old daughter Grace drove out to discuss a few final details with the contractor. She was crossing a busy highway and didn't see the car that was barreling down the road straight at her. At the last minute Mary Sue hit her brakes. The driver of the other car turned and avoided hitting her broadside, but the impact of the collision carried both cars over an embankment on the other side of the road.

I was in Columbus teaching a class on the OSU campus, attending a graduate class I was enrolled in, and scheduled to teach late Bible classes that night. At noon someone came into my midday class and told me that Mary Sue had been in an accident and I needed to call the hospital. I spoke to a nurse, who said, "Now, don't get excited. Your wife and daughter are okay, but they're here in the hospital and you need to come on up here."

I got into my car and drove the seventy miles back to Mansfield as fast as I figured was safe—or maybe faster. At the hospital I found that Mary Sue and Grace were not okay, but fortunately, their injuries weren't life threatening. Grace had a mild concussion and had been unconscious for a little while; Mary Sue had a mild concussion and severe whiplash, the effects of which she's lived with ever since. When I saw her, she was in a neck brace and had been unconscious for a few hours. By the grace of God, they both recovered over the next few weeks.

Since I'd just resigned from Crusade, we had no medical insurance and no idea how we were going to pay the medical bills. But when Bill Bright learned about our situation, he kept me on staff temporarily so we could use Campus Crusade benefits to pay our medical bills. I'll always be grateful for that.

When we finally moved to Grace Haven Farm that Thanksgiving, we didn't have much food to put on the table. What little furniture we had was in pretty poor condition. As always, we trusted in God to provide, and as always, He did, although in a roundabout way.

Mary Sue's accident had totaled the car. I traded it in for another station wagon—we needed station wagons because we already had four children. One winter day that year, Mary Sue forgot to put the car in park when she got out to take groceries into the house. Our house was on a hill, and the car rolled down it, smashed through a sturdy fence constructed to keep Hod's horses near their barn, and ran up onto a huge pile of dirt left over from some construction work. There it sat, battered and perched on the mound of frozen soil. The good news—which came some time later—was that the insurance company gave us a very nice settlement. I was able to buy a less expensive station wagon, and we used the rest of the money to live on.

Some years before, I had been drawn to a book titled *Hudson Taylor's Spiritual Secret.* Taylor was the founder of the China Inland Mission, which became the largest Protestant missionary movement in China. I was captivated by the story. One of the things that most appealed to me was that Taylor relied exclusively on God to support his ministry. He never took collections at services or made fundraising appeals. He prayed in faith, and somehow God sent him the funds he needed. Now God was giving Mary Sue and me the opportunity to do the same thing. We had no church to support us; we had no official organization. I did form a little group called Grace Fellowship of Mansfield, which was incorporated by a lawyer friend of ours as a vehicle through which people could give. The people in my Columbus Bible classes were worried about us and wanted to support us.

"Why don't you take any offerings?" they asked.

I said, "If God wants us to have money, he'll supply it."

They took their cue from that and quickly formed an organization called Layman's Challenge, which received funds from people who attended my Bible classes. Layman's Challenge made no appeals, and we had no guarantee of how much we'd have to live on. Although financially insecure, we were immensely thankful for this kind of support.

Grace Haven Farm proved to be the perfect place for our growing youth work. The Boleskys let us use all the facilities on the farm as well as the workers' recreation center at the Therm-O-Disc factory two or three miles away. Students at Ohio State and the other universities in Ohio who had come to know about us joined local high-school seniors for retreats that began on Friday evening and ended with a worship service in our big basement on Sunday morning.

We'd been at the farm for about a year and a half when Ray Nethery joined us. Ray, a former vice president of Campus Crusade, was one of my closest friends. He had resigned from Crusade before I did and was an active member of our study group. The Boleskys built a big, beautiful house for Ray and his family on the hill above our house.

I enjoyed having Ray with us; it was good to talk to someone who shared the questions and concerns that had led to our departure from Crusade. But there were also some significant differences between our views. Before coming to Mansfield, Ray had spent a year at L'Abri, Francis Schaeffer's community in Switzerland. I'd also made a couple of trips to L'Abri, but the atmosphere there didn't appeal to me. L'Abri had a more philosophical approach to Christian faith. I believed very deeply that our Bible-centered teaching was what the young people who came to us really needed. We agreed to disagree.

MY WORK ON THE FARM didn't keep me from being affected by the events that were rocking the country in 1970. On May 4 of that year, four students were killed at Kent State University, 140 miles northeast of Columbus. Students across the country reacted immediately. At Ohio State, students blocked the entrances to a number of university buildings. The next day they attacked the university president's house and the administration building.

I was on campus for my graduate courses and Bible teaching when the riots started. It was a chilling experience, but it was also a chance to share Christ. I rounded up a group of men I worked with, picked up some pamphlets on 1 Corinthians 13 (St. Paul's beautiful discourse on love), and distributed them to the students who were planning the disturbances. I was well known on campus as the former director of Crusade and the organizer of Operation Other Side, and the students weren't happy to see me at their meeting. Nonetheless, we felt at the time that our witness helped to defuse the growing confrontation.

STUDENTS AND MEMBERS of our Bible classes weren't the only people to whom we were ministering. "Hippies" began to show up on our doorstep: long-haired, somewhat unkempt kids with packs on their backs. This was the height of the Jesus People movement, and thousands of young people were hitchhiking their way all over America. They were newly filled with a love for Jesus, eager to study the Bible and pass the Word on to others. Hundreds of them found their way to the farm; some stayed on for a while, but most were only passing through. Usually our visitors crashed on our basement floor because we didn't have many extra beds. Between the visitors and our weekend retreats, we began to run short of space. We split them up: the guys slept in the nice-sized basement in the Netherys' house while the girls stayed with us. Hod had a large new barn with a small riding arena inside for his horses, and guys often slept in the hayloft.

Of course, some of the folks floating through weren't really Jesus people at all. They were hippies looking for a commune to join or a place to crash. Many were drug users or had other serious problems. We did our best to bring them to Christ. Sadly, we had to ask those beyond our help to leave. But others managed to turn their lives around.

The continuing influx of young transients baffled me. *Where are these people coming from?* I wondered. *How did they know we were here?* It wasn't until the end of our time in Mansfield that I found out a book titled *The Jesus People* listed Grace Haven Farm as one of the places in central Ohio where kids could drop in. Early on, a young man had come to us who said he wanted to write a paper about our work; he turned out to be a research assistant for one of the professors who wrote that book.

Mary Sue's care and concern for our guests was a wonder in itself. Hospitality and creativity seemed to come naturally to her. One weekend, almost 200 kids showed up for a retreat. There was no fee; all they had to do was bring their own food. Mary Sue took the strange assortment of items the kids had brought in their backpacks and made it into edible dishes. It wasn't the miracle of the loaves and fishes, but she managed to make that food last all weekend.

IN SPITE OF ALL THE ACTIVITY at Grace Haven Farm, I continued my quest to find out more about the ancient church. I was teaching the Book of Acts, and again I felt that the church of the apostles was very different from the church I knew. When I first began to explore this issue, I'd compared the church in Antioch to the church I was pastoring in Xenia. Now, as I went through Acts again verse by verse, my unease grew.

We were attending a little Baptist church in Mansfield—after all, I was an ordained Baptist minister—but I was becoming convinced that wasn't enough. What I found in the New Testament, in Paul's letters as well as in Acts, were house churches. I thought that was the way we'd have to go. The kids who came to the farm wouldn't go to church; they kept asking me to hold services at home.

But we didn't do that right away. Then one day my children came to me and said, "Dad, we're not getting anything out of Sunday school." The Mansfield church had a small congregation, and their Sunday school wasn't very well organized. "You can preach and teach. Why don't we have church here?"

"Why don't we have communion here?" my son Tom added.

For a while I resisted. And then I thought, *Here in Mansfield I've got the freedom to have communion every Sunday.* It was clearly taught in the New Testament that Christ had commanded this; to do it was a matter of obedience.

Eventually I said, "Okay, we will. But if we do, we're going to do it the way the New Testament church did. We're going to have communion every Sunday." We used our large basement as a place to meet. Students, Jesus People, hippies, Bible class members: we all shared the Lord's Supper. The first time I held the service there was the first time I'd ever celebrated communion outside a church. I wondered if I'd be struck by lightning.

In those days in Mansfield, I felt the importance of the Lord's Supper, but I hardly understood it. As a Baptist, I'd been brought up to see the elements, the bread and wine, as mere symbols: they reminded us of what Christ had done for us. We held a communion service quarterly, but what we thought of as the meat of our service was praying, singing, and preaching.

As I learned more about the ancient church and the teachings of the great fathers who shepherded it, I came to see that the church has always understood the Lord's Supper as so much more. It is the center of the church. In it Christ comes to us not just as a memory but truly to feed us, body and spirit, with His Body and Blood. I didn't know all that then, but I knew that quarterly communion wasn't enough.

MARY SUE AND I LOVED our four years at Grace Haven Farm. Some truly amazing things happened there. Take Chuck Batsch, for instance. Chuck was the son of Barbara Batsch, a longtime participant in my Bible studies in Columbus and Mansfield, and her husband Frank. Chuck was a rebellious fifteen-year-old with a truckful of problems. The Batsches were heartsick, worried about where their son was going to end up. I offered to have Chuck live with us for a few months. He wasn't very happy with us at first, but we firmly yet lovingly insisted that he follow the rules of the farm, which included doing a good day's work. Slowly but surely his heart softened, and before he left us he had accepted Christ and cleaned up his life. I baptized him in the trout-stocked pond the Boleskys had built on the property.

Every baptism is a little miracle, but there are twenty-seven of them I'll never forget. It was the end of February, and we had a particularly enthusiastic group at a retreat. After the concluding Sunday-evening service, everyone came over to our house for popcorn. We had about a hundred people in a space that could comfortably accommodate seventy-five—standing.

A cold northern wind blew in and snow fell in sheets out of the north. One of the boys—Bob, the brother of Herb McCollum's wife, Kathy—who had been on a retreat the year before came up to me and said, "Gordon, I had planned to have you baptize us while we were here. I brought two other guys whom I led to Christ during the retreat last year, and all three of us want to be baptized."

I said, "Bob, that's a good idea, but it's snowing out there. It's going to be so cold by tomorrow morning that the pond we use for baptisms will be frozen over, and we really won't be able to do it. Why don't you all come back in the spring? I'll be glad to baptize you then."

"I really want to be baptized," Bob said. "Can't we just be baptized tonight?"

What could I say? I certainly didn't want to discourage these young men.

We were tightly jammed into the room, with about two inches of popcorn covering the floor. Joan, a student at Ohio State who'd been involved in our work for some time, was standing nearby.

"I heard what you were talking about," Joan said. "I want to be baptized, too."

I said, "Joan, first of all, you're a Catholic. Your parents are not going to like it if I baptize you."

Joan said, "My parents consider me old enough to make my own decisions."

"Well, if you're confident about that, I'll include you in the baptism," I said.

Now you can't talk in a situation like that without being overheard. Three other students said, "We want to be baptized too."

Finally I said, "Okay. I'll go upstairs and put on extra clothes. If you've brought any extra clothes with you, go get them and put them on, and we'll go down to the pond and I'll baptize you."

It was close to midnight, but we had a large floodlight on the pond, so we had no trouble seeing. By the time I reached the top of the stairs, pushing my way through students to get to our bedroom for warm clothing, seven or eight more kids had asked to be baptized. I knew them all well enough to believe their faith was genuine, so I said okay.

When I went into the bedroom, Mary Sue, who was pregnant with our daughter Jacqueline, said, "What are you doing?"

"I'm putting on more clothes because I've been asked to baptize some kids down at the pond."

"Have you lost your mind?"

That was a very good question. It was nearly midnight and snowing at an unbelievable pace. "Well, I couldn't talk them out of it," I said. That was the only answer I could give.

So I put on some long johns, an extra pair of pants, and a bomber jacket. I thought all that would keep me warm while I was waiting for the kids to arrive. I went down to the pond and stood there shivering as I watched the kids pour out of our house and out of the Netherys' house and the barn. Word had spread, and a crowd of kids gathered at the pond. They sang beautiful baptismal songs while we waited for everybody to get ready.

When I was ready to go into the water, Star McClendon, a young African-American man who had worked with us at Ohio

State, said, "Gordon, you're going to need some help. Do you want me to help you?"

I'd had surgery on New Year's Day that year, so I said, "Thank you. I do need help." We plunged into the pond. As we walked into it, I broke through a skin of ice and kicked little shards out of the way. I brought the first person in—it was Bob—and as I immersed him, I said, "In the name of the Father, the Son, and the Holy Spirit." I looked up at the crowd and said, "I can't wait for those of you who are expecting to be baptized to come in one at a time." I couldn't breathe in that icy water; I felt like I'd been cut in two with a machete. "You can all come in now." After the third baptism I looked up and saw the water full of people. *If they're willing to walk into this frigid water and be baptized,* I thought, *I am going to do it.* Before it was over, I'd baptized twenty-seven people in that driving snowstorm.

One of them was a boy Mary Sue and I had thrown off the farm that same day. He'd brought marijuana with him and was offering it to the other kids. The local juvenile judge had threatened to close the farm down because he suspected drugs were being used on the premises. So we told the boy he had to leave immediately.

"I didn't mean to cause any problems," he said.

Mary Sue and I said, "We don't care—you're leaving now." We put him in the car, took him out to the freeway, and told him to hitch a ride back to Columbus. Lo and behold, that night he was in the water wanting to be baptized.

I said, "What are you doing here?"

"I came in . . . I was . . . I stayed in the back of the room tonight," he answered. We'd had a meeting at the recreation center where kids, beginning with Bob, had given their testimonies about coming to Christ. "I've given my heart to Christ."

"Okay. In the name of the Father, of the Son, and of the Holy Spirit," I said, and under he went. That young man is now a deacon at an Orthodox church in Alabama.

From the group we baptized that night came the leaders of campus Bible classes throughout central Ohio. And two megachurches in Columbus had their beginning that night.

DESPITE ALL THE SPIRITUAL FRUITS that blessed our ministry, we knew we still hadn't discovered the New Testament church—not yet. We had many of the elements of what we thought the church was, but something was still missing. Frankly, I didn't know what it was. We were on our own, not a part of any larger church structure. I was making decisions by myself; I had no one in authority over me. There was a lot more I needed to learn.

With the facilities we had on the farm and at the Therm-O-Disc recreation center, we had a perfect venue for conferences. So in the summer, we invited many of the people who'd left Campus Crusade to speak: Peter Gillquist, Jon Braun, Richard Ballew, Jack Sparks, and Ken Berven, among others. People came in droves to our weeklong conferences. They brought campers and tents and stayed outside. And the topic was always the church: What is the church? Where is it?

At our second conference we invited Hal Lindsay—who would later write the mega-bestseller *The Late, Great Planet Earth*—to speak. Hal and his wife, Jan, had driven a camper to Mansfield from Los Angeles.

"There's a Bible conference coming up next weekend in Nashville, Tennessee," Hal told me, "and they've asked me to come. The people down there want me to start Bible classes for them. But I'm not ready to move from L.A. Would you come along with us and be one of the teachers?"

After thinking over Hal's request, I said yes. On the next Wednesday I rode to Nashville with Hal and Jan.

The conference was held in a hotel on Harding Place, south of the city. I guess I impressed the people there, because they asked me to come and teach them.

I had a real sense of being called to Nashville. It seemed like the right time. Although Ray Nethery and I were still friends, our disagreement about the future of Grace Haven had widened. Ray had brought in another man to help him who got between Ray and me, and the ministry seemed to be going in a different direction from the one I wanted. At the same time, I felt Ray deserved the opportunity to be his own man.

If we went to Nashville, we would again be making a huge transition, just four years after coming to the farm. Mary Sue and I talked to the children. "We believe God is leading us to go down there," we said. "It seems the door is open."

We were getting ready to pack our things to move when I walked by our seven-year-old daughter Grace's bedroom. She was sitting on the bed crying. "Honey, what are you crying about?" I asked.

"I don't want to move to Nashville," she said.

"But it's a nice place and there are nice people, and we'll have a—we're going to find a place to live. You'll really like it in Nashville. It's very pretty there."

"But Daddy," she said, "I don't want to learn to speak Southern!"

Grace wasn't the only one who didn't want to go to Nashville. Our son Tom begged to stay. He was going to the Christian high school in Mansfield, where he played both soccer and basketball. His coach—who was also the principal of the school and our neighbor on the farm—put on a full-court press to keep him in school. Tom was a good player, but he was just a little aggressive. He was their hatchet man: he fouled out more than any other player on the basketball team. Finally I gave in and agreed that Tom could spend his junior and senior years living under the guidance of the principal in Mansfield while the rest of the family was in Nashville.

So our family moved to Nashville, and four single young people agreed to come with us to help. We drove a big moving truck, with three cars and a smaller truck following along. All of us wound up in a farmhouse in Bon Aqua, Tennessee, and that began a whole new stage of our life.

CHAPTER 6

Tennessee and the NCAO

W E ARRIVED IN Bon Aqua, Tennessee, in mid-July, 1972. The house we lived in temporarily was a two-bedroom farmhouse with a creek in front that filled easily and once trapped us in the house for a day and a half when the creek was swollen by heavy rains. We couldn't all fit in the small farmhouse—four young people who came down with us, four of our five children, and Mary Sue and me—so we found space for two girls with people we'd already met in Nashville.

Our house was full of boxes, so we held church on the wide porch that first Sunday. I met with our friends in Nashville later that week to figure out where our family was going to settle. We had to know where to register our children for school before the first of September. During the discussion someone asked, "Where did you go to church on Sunday?"

"Well," I answered, "we had church in Bon Aqua on the front porch of the house."

"Oh," he said, somewhat startled and a little curious. These friends of ours lived in a modest house in Belle Meade, one of the wealthiest neighborhoods in the city, so I was surprised when the next question was, "Could we come out next Sunday?"

"Remember," I replied, "that you'll have to ford the creek to get to the house. So pray the creek doesn't rise!" It didn't, and they did.

The weather was fine that Sunday. We managed to get enough chairs and set them up under a beautiful oak tree in the front yard. We'd bought crackers and grape juice for a communion service. But I was skeptical. "You know," I said to Mary Sue, "I don't know if they'll come or not."

The week before, I'd managed to get in touch with Herb and Kathy McCollum, our close friends from Ohio State. Right after we had decided to go to Nashville, I got a letter from Herb, who was now a veterinarian. "We're getting ready to move to Nashville," he wrote, "and we'll arrive there sometime around the first week in July."

I wrote back to him and said, "Well, that's certainly a coincidence. We're moving to Nashville, and we expect to be down there about the middle of July!"

Herb sent me the name of the veterinary clinic where he was going to work, and when we got to Bon Aqua, I called the clinic and they gave us his address. I went to see Herb and Kathy and told them about our house church. "We'll be at church next Sunday," they told me.

Three carloads of people drove out to our house that Sunday. Besides the McCollums, our little congregation included our friends from Belle Meade Boulevard, an airline pilot and his wife, and another friend with his wife and their children.

After church was over, I told them our problem: Where would we send our children to school if we didn't know where we'd end up living? I wanted a house in Nashville, but I couldn't figure out where to look. Our Belle Meade friend said, "Well, you know, it so happens there's an older house for sale at 525 Belle Meade Boulevard."

I had no idea where that was, and when I found out, I was astonished. Number 525 is in the center of Belle Meade Boulevard, which is the exact geographic center of Belle Meade, a former plantation where race horses had been raised. Now it's one of the wealthiest neighborhoods in Nashville. When I first drove through it, I was bowled over (and a little bit intimidated) by the big houses, with their beautifully trimmed lawns and backyard stands of trees.

"The house is old and needs a lot of work," our friend said. "But I'm going to buy it. It will be a good investment for me and a good place for you to live."

It seemed like a miracle. Here we were in a new city with people we hardly knew and who hardly knew us. We'd already had so many blessings. Just a few years earlier the Boleskys had built us a fine house at Grace Haven Farm. And now God was providing for us again.

The Tudor-style house with its off-white paint was dwarfed by many of the other houses in Belle Meade, but it was more than I could have imagined before seeing it. "Just paint the outside," I said. "Don't do too much inside." I didn't want our friend to invest too much in us. We'd done a lot of moving in the course of our ministry, and we didn't know if God would call us to move again.

A family was living in the house, so we moved into an apartment building next door for the three months they'd be staying there. Our apartment was very small, and I don't think the elderly people who lived in the building were happy to see us move in with our whole crew. When the house was finally vacant, our friend had the outside painted and had some repairs done inside as well, working around our family and guests.

Once we settled in, we transferred our home church to our living room. One Sunday we saw some unfamiliar faces; one of the men who had worshiped with us in Bon Aqua had invited friends to our living-room service. They liked what they saw. One of them said, "My grandmother lives a block away from here, but she's too old to come on Sundays. Could we take the church to her?"

One of the advantages of a house church is mobility. We went over to the man's grandmother's house to hold a service. She had a much larger living room, and we ended up worshiping there as long as we lived on Belle Meade Boulevard. Our congregation of prosperous Tennesseans was very different from the students and Jesus People we'd worked with at Grace Haven Farm, but we did the same things we had done there. We sang hymns (more traditional ones), I taught the Bible, and we served communion.

I'd been asked to come to Nashville to take over a Bible class, so I began to teach on Tuesday nights. The class began to grow, and soon I was teaching in other homes throughout Nashville. Eventually the classes grew so large that we had to move them out of people's homes to the high school auditorium. Mary Sue and I made many close and dear friends among our Bible students. One of them even built a "Gordon Walker Room" in his basement for our classes. Because we had no church to provide support, we formed Grace Ministries, a vehicle for accepting gifts to support our work. Grace Ministries provided absolutely crucial support for our work in the years that followed.

The attendees at the Bible studies included some of the wealthiest people in Nashville. On Sundays they went to large, fashionable churches they had no intention of leaving. But after a while, some of the Belle Meade people decided they'd like me to be their pastor as well as their teacher. They wanted to start a nondenominational Bible church. The friend who owned the house on Belle Meade Boulevard that we lived in for five and a half years also owned a large plot (about four acres) which she offered as a site for our church. But for all our success with the Bible studies, I was still struggling in prayer and study to find the New Testament church, and pastoring another Protestant church was not what I thought the Lord wanted me to be doing. He was leading me to the New Testament church, and at that point in my journey the small house churches were as close as I had come to understanding what that meant. I knew I had further to go.

I also had more to learn about ways the Lord could make his will known to me. Over the years the Lord has spoken to me in many ways, most often with a persistent thought or a soft voice, sometimes a gentle nudge. But He has occasionally spoken aloud to me, as on this occasion when we lived in Belle Meade.

The story involves a beautiful but unhappy woman named Nancy who had started attending our Bible study. She had even done some work for me, typing my letters at no charge. She was recently divorced from her wealthy husband and simply could not deal with her sadness.

One day while I was cutting the grass I heard a firm voice say, "Go see Nancy." I thought, "I only have five swaths to cut, and I'll go then." The voice said, "Go see Nancy NOW!"

I raced to her apartment and parked directly in front. Fortunately she saw me arrive. As I ran up the stairs I could hear her wailing in anguish. She said, "I was sitting on the bed with the gun in my hand getting ready to shoot myself when I saw your car pull up." I talked to her at length and explained that I had been ordered to come by the Lord Himself. Had I waited a few more minutes, I believe she would have been dead. This reassurance of the Lord's personal concern for her helped her to get her life straightened out, and she had no more thoughts of self-injury.

To me the lesson of this encounter was that we must listen to the Lord, however He speaks to us; we must listen . . . and ACT!

SINCE OUR DAYS AT GRACE HAVEN FARM, my ex–Campus Crusade friends and I had been holding periodic Bible study conferences. Some of these were held in Nashville, and some were in places where the other men had started house churches of their own. The intensive Bible study we did for those conferences drew us closer together. It also gave us a deeper sense of where we were going as well as principles for keeping our house churches on the right track. In retrospect, these periodic Bible study conferences were the precursors to the Weekend Institute of Biblical Theology used in the Evangelical Orthodox Church in years to come.

I arranged to hold a conference at the Vanderbilt University law school with presentations by some of my friends formerly of Campus Crusade: Peter Gillquist (who came to town in a ten-gallon hat, boots, and blue jeans), Jon Braun, Jack Sparks, Ken Berven, and Ray Nethery. On that Saturday night the auditorium was packed.

Jack Sparks, who years before had organized the Christian

Liberation Front (a Jesus People group in Berkeley), preached on the evils of wealth, which he called "the great curse of America." The problem of wealth and poverty in America had become a focus of discussion in the country at large, and Jack had just read a bestselling book on the subject. I agreed with most of what he said, but he said it in a very contentious way. Many of the people who attended my Bible classes were in the audience, and many of them were wealthy. They felt wounded by what Jack was saying.

I got up and tried to smooth things over. "I understand what you're saying," I said to Jack, "but can't we use wealth in a positive way? Don't the wealthy have the opportunity to assist the poor and advance the kingdom of God?" Jack held his ground: "Scripture is clear: Jesus says in Matthew 19:24, 'It is easier for a camel to go through the eye of a needle than for a rich man to enter the kingdom of God.'"

Peter Gillquist dubbed that night my Black Saturday. After that, although my core of friends stood by me, my Bible classes in Nashville were essentially finished. I was devastated. I began to feel isolated, cut off from so many who had been touched by my teaching. I had been working hard to take care of my family and put food on the table, and now I'd inadvertently alienated many of the people who'd been supporting me. I felt the same loss as when I left Xenia, Campus Crusade, and Mansfield: like the boy who'd put those wooden bullets on the rock altar in Palmerdale so many years before. It was a long time before I realized that only by sacrificing the familiar, comfortable paths could I find the road to the New Testament church and the fullness of faith.

ONCE I WAS NO LONGER TEACHING the Bible classes, I decided to put my energy into our house church. Despite the difficulties Black Saturday had caused, the house church began to grow. In time I divided it into seven churches. Through my study of Acts and the letters of Paul, I'd come to believe the small house church, with just a few families, was the New Testament model. And a number of people in our church were ready to take up leadership positions in churches of their own. Eventually I was responsible for seven house churches in the Nashville area and five or six house churches in widely scattered areas, including other states.

As our ministry grew, people who had been with us at Grace Haven Farm moved to Nashville to be closer to us. They shared houses and apartments and formed a tight-knit community. And as we had in Ohio, we took in young people who needed guidance to get their lives together. We were trying as hard as we could to live the New Testament model of Christian life as we understood it—following the lead of the Holy Spirit, worshiping together every Sunday, sharing our gifts and our burdens, reading deeply in the Scriptures, and sharing the gospel with others.

IN THE SUMMER OF 1973, seventy men who were mostly veterans of Campus Crusade met in Dallas, Texas, where the Christian Booksellers Association was holding its annual convention. We spent the week in intense discussions about the house churches we were founding. What kind of leadership would they have? How would they worship? How many families did they need to be viable? What relationship should they have with each other?

With the approval of the larger group, a smaller group of us decided to meet regularly to discuss our churches and their relationship to the church of the New Testament. A few months later, we met at Jack Sparks' house in Berkeley. Our group didn't have a lot of things in common, but we did share one passion—the search for the real New Testament church. We were starting to realize how little we really knew about it. The question of authority in the church was particularly important to us. How were our house churches going to be kept together? Who would decide what should be taught and what should be done? Six of us—the older men—were appointed elders to guard the churches: Jack Sparks, Jon Braun, Dick Ballew, Ray Nethery, Ken Berven, and I.

Peter Gillquist had moved to a country home in Jackson, Tennessee, northeast of Memphis, and we met there with a group of house-church leaders in January, 1974. It was a contentious meeting. The other men hadn't stayed together the way we had; each of them was on his own journey and had his own idea of what our direction should be. At the end of the week, the other five elders and I went to a hotel in Memphis for a postmortem.

Someone said, "We need Pete Gillquist here. He's been the catalyst of our discussions." So we invited him to meet with us and asked him to join the group. That made seven of us. We decided there was too much contention, too much debate at our meetings. So we decided not to have public conferences for the time being. Instead, our core group started meeting four times a year. We'd get someone to let us use a vacation home, a retreat center, or some other place where we could spend a week together.

"Everybody says they're the ancient church," Jack Sparks said at one of our first meetings. "We need to find out who's right."

Jack brought a different perspective to our group. He hadn't been brought up as an evangelical in the Bible Belt, and he had the research skills and analytical ability of a well-trained academic. "I think we should start from the beginning and take a fresh, close look at the New Testament. Then we've got to find out what happened to that Church between the death of the last apostle and the beginning of the Reformation."

I thought Jack's last point was crucial. As a Baptist, I'd never thought much about the ancient church. After the apostles died, I assumed everything went dark. By the second century, I believed, the church had turned away from its Lord. My seminary studies hadn't helped much; our church history classes whizzed through the millennium and a half between the New Testament and the Reformation. I knew enough church history to know that after the apostles died, the early church went on to make thousands of new converts, many of whom witnessed to their faith by dying for it. Surely it took the power of God to do that. "What was really going on in the ancient church?" I asked. "How did it turn into the apostate church that existed in Luther's day?"

Jon Braun had the same question. "How long," he asked, "did the church remain faithful?"

We had so much ground to cover that we divided up the work among the seven of us. Peter would coordinate our research. Jack took on the topic of worship in the early church. Jon looked at church history as a whole. Dick tackled the church's doctrine. Ken studied the pre-Reformation church, and Ray volunteered to cover the post-Reformation era.

"That's all very well," I said, "but what really counts is Scripture. "I'm going to take everything you report and check it against the Bible. Anything that doesn't agree with the Bible is out."

Jack felt it was important for us to look at the original sources from the times we were studying rather than relying on textbooks or some scholar's opinion. He'd been reading the church fathers, the leaders and thinkers who lived during the period from the end of the apostolic age to the Middle Ages. He sent us sheaves of material he'd collected for the rest of us to read. The fathers were new to me, and I was deeply touched by them. Their writings were windows into a world I'd scarcely known existed, and they became the door to a richer, more joyful Christian life.

The following summer we met in a cold, damp cabin at Friday Harbor in the San Juan Islands off the northwest Washington coast so we could share what we'd been learning. At our first session, Jack Sparks said, "Well, men, I've got good news and bad news. The good news is that worship was the focus of the ancient church."

That wasn't news to me. The Bible is clear about worship; just read the second chapter of Acts: "They continued steadfastly in the apostles' doctrine and fellowship, in the breaking of bread, and in prayers" (Acts 2:42). "So continuing daily with one accord in the temple, and breaking bread from house to house, they ate their food with gladness and simplicity of heart, praising God and having favor with all the people. And the Lord added to the church daily those who were being saved" (Acts 2:46–47).

"Now the bad news," Jack said, "is that there's been liturgy—a set order of worship—from the very beginning."

That really was bad news to me. *Liturgy* was one of the words I'd use if I felt like cussing. We Southern Baptists didn't want any part of it—we believed in worshiping the Lord spontaneously, with no set prayers. (It was only later that I realized Baptist services generally followed their own set pattern, if not in the same words. We actually had a liturgy of our own.)

Jack told us that one of the earliest of the fathers, Justin Martyr (c. AD 150), had described Christian worship as it existed in his time. The liturgy was divided into two parts, the *synaxis* (gathering or assembly), which consisted of hymns, Scripture readings, and a sermon; and the *Eucharist* (thanksgiving), which was made up of prayers of intercession, the collection of the people's offerings, and communion. The same pattern was described by other early fathers. And before them, the *Didache,* a document that comes from the earliest years of the church, was a witness to the regular celebration of the Eucharist.

The Scriptures were full of liturgical worship: in the synagogue, where the Word of God was read and taught, and in the temple, where God was worshiped with song and sacrifice. Jack traced this pattern of worship through the New Testament, from Jesus' proclamation of the words of Isaiah in the synagogue (Luke 4:16–30) to the heavenly worship in Revelation 4 and 5.

That night I lay in my sleeping bag thinking, *Why did he have to bring this up?* I had confidence in Jack's intellect and his ability as a researcher, but I didn't like what he had found.

It took a while for this bitter pill to go down, but the more I studied the long paper Jack had written and compared his findings to the Bible, the more I realized he was right. Liturgy is a part of worship: the Jews followed a liturgy; Jesus participated in liturgy; the disciples used it; the ancient church continued the ritual. I had to accept that reality, and that would mean some dramatic changes in the way we worshiped in our house churches.

There were other things Jack had touched on that disturbed me. Foremost among these was that the church fathers had taught from the very beginning that the bread and wine of the Eucharist were somehow (they never explained how) the real Body and Blood of Christ. As a Baptist I'd believed that the communion bread and wine (or grape juice) were only symbols to help us remember Jesus. It took a while before I could accept that ancient teaching; I don't think anyone on this earth can truly understand it.

Two of the other reports also made me uneasy. Jon Braun's survey of church history focused on the place of bishops in the church. "Three orders of ministry, bishops (*episcopoi*), elders (*presbyteroi*), and deacons (*diakinoi*), go all the way back to the beginning of the church," he said. Bishops ruled the churches. The twelve apostles, ordained by Jesus himself (John 20:22), were the first bishops: at the Council of Jerusalem (reported in Acts 15) the apostle James, Bishop of Jerusalem, authoritatively resolves the question of Gentiles in the church. Paul writes about bishops in his letters, in Philippians 4:3 and more fully in 1 Timothy 3. Ignatius, the second successor of the apostle Peter as Bishop of Antioch, wrote extensively about the office of bishop in the letters he wrote to the churches in the early second century when he was on the way to his martyrdom. Born in about AD 69, the martyr Polycarp had been consecrated as Bishop of Smyrna by the apostle John. The bishop was the source of unity in his church.

Jon stressed the need for authority in the church. Even denominations that reject the office of bishop have someone in charge. I could see the truth in that; even the Southern Baptists had the Southern Baptist Convention to coordinate the work of the individual congregations. But on the other hand, Baptists stressed the independence of each local church. I was suspicious of centralized authority. Was it safe to surrender the power to govern a group of local churches to one man? Wouldn't this subject the elders and their congregations to his fallible judgment, or even to his whims?

Jon then explained more about the history of the church and how the original, united church had split apart in 1054 into Eastern and Western churches. One of the key issues in the dispute was the Nicene Creed, the product of the earliest church councils. When it described the Holy Spirit, the creed read, "Who proceeds from the Father," repeating the words of Jesus in John 15:26: "But when the Helper comes, whom I shall send to you from the Father, the Spirit of truth who proceeds from the Father, He will testify of Me." The Western church had added the Latin term *filioque*, "and the Son," so that the Western version came to say, "I believe in the Holy Spirit, who proceeds from the Father and the Son." It was clear that the East had retained the ancient and scriptural wording, while the West had changed it. Through further studies in the next few years, we came to see the grave damage done to our understanding of the Holy Trinity by this unauthorized change in the wording of the Nicene Creed.

Dick Ballew's report centered on the many disputes about doctrine in the early church. Most of them were about the nature and person of Christ: Is He a creature, or is He God? What is the relationship between the man Jesus and the eternal Son? Was Jesus a human indwelt by God, or God pretending to be human, or both human and divine? And if the last was true, how are His human and divine natures related?

When disagreements like these threatened the faith as it had been handed down, they were resolved by an ecumenical (universal) council that was made up of the bishops from the local churches. The council produced a definition of what the Scriptures taught about the controversy and what the church had believed about it from the beginning. Those who followed the council's doctrine were called orthodox ("right believing"; literally "right praising"), while those who didn't were heretics (those who choose their own way). While in council, the bishops of the church were exercising authority over all the churches.

I wasn't the only one who found it hard to digest these reports. There was dismay and spirited debate about each of them. But the evidence seemed overwhelming. I left the meeting determined to continue praying and searching the Scriptures until I was convinced I had the answers.

One of our following meetings was held on Padre Island, off the east coast of Texas. Some friends of Ken Berven let us use their vacation home there. Again we faced the question of authority. We decided we weren't providing enough direction to our house churches. We didn't have any real authority, so how could we ask people to follow us? We needed to define governing principles to guide us in leading the churches. So we formulated the following:

1. **Grace:** God deals with us according to His grace. We are grateful recipients of this grace and are called to reflect it in the world.

2. **True Community:** We are committed to the Lord and each other in a local church, fully reconciled and involved in every

aspect of one another's lives. We are diligent to resolve anything that might cloud our relationship with God or each other.

3. **Vision:** We are called to be a light shining in darkness and to be a living demonstration of the blessing and order of God's reign as we live in our own local and cultural setting.

4. **Authoritative, Serving Leadership:** We have a government overseen by elders and participated in by the people, expressing together the will of God on earth.

5. **Care:** The church is called to look after the needs of its people in all areas, including financial, emotional, spiritual, and vocational.

6. **Seeing and Hearing from God:** The Holy Spirit enables all Christians to see and hear from Him, and the Spirit leads them. It is the role of the church to determine when God has in fact spoken and to obey accordingly.

7. **Good Works:** We are committed to put love into action collectively and individually, preaching the gospel and caring for the sick, the poverty-stricken, and the troubled.

8. **Godliness:** We are committed to living in ways that express the holiness to which God has called His people.

9. **Orthodox Theology:** We believe, confess, and teach only those doctrines that are found in the Scriptures and are in keeping with the ancient formulations of the ecumenical councils of the church. We categorically reject novel doctrines.

10. **Worship:** The very heart of our worship of the Triune God

is the Holy Eucharist. In keeping with this ancient orthodox view, we are seeking to capture once again a true spirit of worship among God's people.

11. **The Blessed Hope:** We look forward to the Second Advent of Christ the King and to our participation in the eternal Kingdom that He will fully establish at the end of this age.

12. **Catholicity:** We are a part of the One Holy Catholic and Apostolic Church and are eager to establish fellowship with all others who are a part of it as well. The church is *catholic* because it teaches the same faith everywhere and at all times; it is *apostolic* because it holds fast to the teaching of the apostles and is governed by their successors.

As we agreed to affirm only "orthodox theology" (above, #9), we spelled orthodoxy with a small "o," but we were beginning to learn about Orthodoxy with a capital O—the Orthodox Church—from our readings in church history and the church fathers. I wasn't ready for that; I still had a Protestant mindset, and I wasn't yet ready for Orthodox theology and practice—the use of icons, the role of Mary, the elaborate liturgy.

We drew our individual churches into a fellowship called the New Covenant Apostolic Order (NCAO), committed to the New Testament church and the faith and practice of the apostles. We now had a structure with which to bring unity to our house churches and share the results of our studies. That was an important step in our journey because it gave us a stronger bond, and we committed ourselves to be a part of the NCAO.

I had a very tense meeting with our church in Nashville when I came back from Padre Island. Some people were unhappy about the decision to have strong leadership, and they were unhappy that I would be serving as their elder. Some of them were ready to leave. But we managed to hang together. To me it appeared things were going well until one of the men decided he wanted his house church to go in a totally different direction. Even though I was their senior elder, there was little I could do to keep our churches together.

IN 1977, TWO OF our most significant ventures had their beginning. That year Jack Sparks moved to Isla Vista, California, where the University of California at Santa Barbara is located. Richard Ballew and Jon Braun were already there. Richard and Jon worked as house painters for a couple of years because their house church wasn't able to support them. With the agreement of the rest of us, Jack and Richard Ballew began the Academy of Orthodox Theology in Isla Vista. The idea was to continue our investigation of Orthodoxy and to provide a seminary-level education to the leaders of our house churches. The academy was necessary to provide the intellectual heft to support the introduction of truly Orthodox faith and practice.

In order to provide us with a platform to communicate what we were learning to our church members and spread our message to a wider Christian public, we founded Conciliar Press (now known as Ancient Faith Publishing). It was the brainchild of Ken Berven, under whose direction it grew and prospered. Conciliar Press published books and pamphlets outlining our beliefs and practices. It also published *Again*, which started out as a tabloid newspaper and grew to be a handsome four-color magazine.

IN LATE 1977 OUR GROUP OF ELDERS gathered in the mountains above Denver, Colorado. We met at the airport, rented a van, and went to the nearest supermarket to buy enough groceries for our stay. Then we went to Wild Basin Lodge and spent the week studying and discussing the Bible, the church fathers, and the theology of the early church. It was the pivotal meeting of the seven of us.

I went into the meeting with a chip on my shoulder about where the group was headed. Dick Ballew started out with an intense presentation on the need for authority in the church. "The New Testament church had the authority of the apostles," he said. "The early church had the authority of their successors, the bishops. Without authority, how can the church hold together? How will it preserve its faith?"

Although I was concerned about the dangers of disunity, as a Baptist, I just didn't believe in authority, and I was getting fired up. "In my view," I said, "authority corrupts and absolute authority corrupts absolutely." The battle was on.

As the debate raged, I found myself more and more uncomfortable. The tone was combative; people seemed to be so attached to their opinions that no compromise was possible. And my Baptist suspicion of authority didn't seem to be widely shared. *I'll go to my room*, I thought, *pack my suitcase, hitchhike back to the Denver airport, and try to get an earlier flight. And I'll never see these men again.*

As I stood up to go, I heard a voice speaking to my spirit—a loud voice. *Sit down*, it said. Just those two words: *Sit down.* That was the distinctive voice I had heard once before in my ministry; listening to it on that occasion had resulted in saving someone's life.

My father brought me up to say "Yes, sir" and "No, sir" and "Yes, ma'am" and "No, ma'am." And I answered in my spirit, *Yes, Sir!* I knew it was the voice of God. I sat down; I dared not leave that room.

Within five minutes, a spirit of peace—the Holy Spirit—came into the room. I knew I belonged here. We didn't have one rancorous discussion from that point on. We became collaborators rather than debaters; we were trying to reach a consensus. How, we asked ourselves, can we have the authority we need to keep our churches together without abusing it?

As the NCAO developed and more people were joining, Jon Braun pressed the issue: "We seven need to make a commitment to one another until death do us part." Making that commitment was vital to us. We agreed that we would follow the truth wherever it led us, no matter what the cost. We committed ourselves to making important decisions only with the blessing of all seven. And it worked for quite a few years.

It was sometimes hard to arrive at agreements, but we learned from the early councils of the church. The early church didn't move forward on theology unless the councils came to consensus. There were always heretics like Arius who refused to submit to the decisions of the councils and had to be turned out of the church. But the church maintained its authority because it had bishops, and those bishops met in councils, whether local or ecumenical (councils of the whole church).

By now, we realized that we had to have bishops in our churches. For some in our Nashville churches, that was just too much. When I'd come back from our quarterly meetings and try to teach what we'd agreed to teach, some of the pastors of our house churches decided they could get along fine without me and the men on the West Coast who were coming up with these strange ideas. "Well, you know," one of our men said, "the West Coast is like a box of cereal that's been turned on its edge. It's all fruits and nuts."

In February 1978, the elders met in Goleta, California, in the building where the academy held its classes. It was pouring rain outside. After we started our discussions, Ray Nethery stood up. "Well, men," he said, "I'm leaving. You guys have become too Catholic for me. I can't agree with you about Communion being Christ's real Body and Blood."

Ray's words broke my heart. Ray and I had been close friends. When our family moved to Nashville, we had handed over the work we had started to Ray and his family. Now we were losing the chance for our churches in Ohio to share this quest. I'd spent twelve-and-a-half years in Ohio—in Xenia, Columbus, and Mansfield—and planted quite a few house churches there. There were churches in Michigan and even on the East Coast that had sprung out of my ministry. When Ray left, he took about two thousand people with him.

Some of the men in our group thought Ray would come back. We had a summer conference planned for Columbus, and before he walked out the door, Ray said, "I'm not canceling that conference. We will have it. And I'll see that it all comes together." But in my heart I knew he wouldn't come back, and he didn't.

We went ahead with the summer conference in Columbus. It was a sad and difficult time. It marked the end of our ties to Ray. For me, it was confirmation that now there was no turning back.

The Walker family at Debbie's wedding to Michael Amick, 1973. Left to right: Mary Sue, Fr. Gordon holding Jacqueline, Debbie, Michael, Grace in front, Tom, Melissa.

CHAPTER 7

Grace Valley Farm

FOR MORE THAN TWO YEARS, Mary Sue and I looked for a farm where we could welcome house-church members and inquirers for intensive study—and some healthful and productive work. I drove all over middle Tennessee looking at farms that I'd found were for sale. It was a discouraging experience. Sometimes I just drove past because the place didn't look right or was obviously too expensive. And whenever I found a farm I liked, the hefty down payment required was far out of our reach.

Then one of the women in our Bible class became bored with her leisurely life and decided to become a realtor. The instructor in her real estate class told her about a farm on Peytonsville Road in Franklin, Tennessee, twenty-two miles from Nashville. "This is the kind of place you should try to sell. It's in a beautiful, up-and-coming area," he said. The woman asked Mary Sue to come and look at the property. Mary Sue loved it.

I was visiting house churches outside Anchorage at the time. The Alaskan churches were led by Harold Dunaway, a colleague back in our days at Campus Crusade. Harold had asked Crusade to send him to Hawaii, but no one in Honolulu would pay his salary. Then a man at an air force base in Alaska said he would sponsor Harold. It's hard to imagine a greater contrast to Honolulu than Anchorage, and Harold was disappointed by the change of plans. But he stuck it out, and his house churches became part of the NCAO. I taught in Alaska for a week, and then went to Saskatchewan, Canada, to visit a church that was struggling. The congregation had difficulties with the direction of the NCAO and had personality conflicts among themselves as well. I persuaded them to stay with us as we pursued the New Testament church.

From Saskatchewan I flew down to Columbus, Ohio, where I met with our old friends Frank and Barbara Batsch. They knew we were looking for a farm because I had been sending out newsletters asking for prayers that God would lead us to a new home for our ministry. Frank and Barbara had already decided what they were going to do before I got there. That night, when we were sitting in their living room, they said, "We know you've been trying to get some money together to buy a farm, so we decided to sell some of our stock to help." They handed me a check for ninety-five thousand dollars!

When I got back from my trip, Mary Sue met me at the Nashville airport and told me how beautiful the farm was that she'd seen. I wanted to see it right away, so we drove straight to Franklin. On the way, I showed Mary Sue the ninety-five-thousand-dollar check. Neither one of us could believe that anyone would give us that much money. If we both liked the place, we'd be able to make an offer.

When we turned off Peytonsville Road, I knew Mary Sue was right. Nestled in a little valley between gently rolling hills, the farm seemed like the perfect place and a worthy successor to Grace Haven Farm. The hundred-year-old farm buildings were in terrible shape, and we'd have to rebuild them. However, the location—surrounded by other farms, quiet and sheltered by the hills, yet close to the city—was exactly what we needed. We'd be able to do the things we'd done back in Ohio: hold retreats for our church members and provide work and shelter for people who looked to deepen their relationship with Christ or straighten out the crooked places in their lives. We deposited the check as soon as we got back to Nashville.

I went back to Franklin a day or two later and asked the owners of the farm what they wanted for it. "We'd be happy to sell it to you for a hundred and forty-five thousand," they said. That was a lot of money in the 1970s, the equivalent of six hundred thousand in today's dollars. I tried my best to negotiate a lower price, but they were adamant. Thanks to the Batsches and God's grace, we had the cash for a down payment. As I thought about the many ways God has saved and sustained us through the years, I realized that we were here at this place and time only by His miracles and grace. So we named the place Grace Valley Farm. We've been there ever since.

When we moved to the farm, our son Tom was a student at Belmont University in Nashville. (After he'd persuaded us to let him stay in Mansfield for high school, I wasn't about to let him go to college outside Tennessee.) He came down to look over the buildings with us, and when he walked into the kitchen, the floor gave way and dropped him two feet into the hole! Termites had done a thorough job, and the house needed a good bit of work. But friends from our house churches came out to replace the floors, including the joists, and to build shelves in the kitchen. It wasn't anything fancy, but at least it was safe, and we could stay there until we could build a house of our own. Looking back now, moving from the middle of Belle Meade to this little run-down farm house was like the Beverly Hillbillies story—but in reverse!

For years Mary Sue and I had wanted to live in a log house, and now we were in a position to fulfill this desire. We planned to build a comfortable two-story house on a ridge above the valley. Again our friends from the house churches, including some who had been with us in Ohio, pitched in to make our dream come true. We've now lived in that house for more than thirty years.

There was plenty of work for church members and guests to do around the farm. We made hay, kept cattle, and even had a horse. A lawyer friend of ours suggested we grow blueberries and sell them. We let people come to pick them, and then Mary Sue weighed and priced them. It was quite a chore, so we came to rely on the blueberry pickers to make donations.

SOMETHING ELSE WAS HAPPENING that summer. Our daughter Melissa had gone to college in Mississippi, where she was seeing a lot of Jon Braun's son Gary, who was there on a football scholarship. Finally Gary proposed to her, and Melissa said yes. The wedding date was set for just about the time we were going to move into our log house.

Somehow things turned out to be a bit more complicated than we expected. The house wasn't finished by the time the wedding came around; the front steps weren't built until a couple of days before. So we had the wedding outside on the farm. We'd built a bathroom upstairs in the farmhouse, and we and the kids slept there. But most of the guests had to sleep outside in sleeping bags. Again God was good—it didn't rain!

DURING OUR FIRST YEARS ON THE FARM, our quest for orthodoxy with a small *o*, the faith and practice of the early church, was gaining momentum. And so was our movement toward Orthodoxy with a capital *O*, that faith and practice as lived today in the Orthodox Church. It was the Academy in Goleta that was giving us impetus. I remember the time Jack Sparks sent me a sheaf of St. Athanasius's letters that he wanted me to copyedit for publication. I walked up and down the gravel path in front of our house with tears in my eyes as I read them. Athanasius was persecuted by his enemies in the church and sent into exile by the emperor. He struggled to preserve the faith of the First Ecumenical Council—which proclaimed that the Son of God took on our humanity, yet is Himself fully God. The faith of Athanasius was my faith. Now the question was not so much where as when; whatever it would cost, I would truly live it.

By 1979 I'd come to the conviction that the Orthodox Church had preserved the faith and structure of the ancient church. I'd gotten over many hurdles, including the liturgy, the four orders of ministry (bishops, presbyters, deacons, and laity), the authority of bishops, the sacraments, and the importance of fasting.

I found deep satisfaction in the Orthodox view of the sacraments, or mysteries, as the Orthodox call them. The seven principal sacraments are (1) baptism, (2) chrismation (anointing with chrism, the Orthodox sacrament of confirmation), (3) confession, (4) Holy Communion, (5) marriage, (6) ordination, and

(7) unction (anointing the sick)—although Orthodoxy doesn't restrict the mysteries to these seven, as the Western church does. Through the power of the Holy Spirit, the mysteries use common physical things—water, chrism, bread, and wine—to begin and strengthen us in our life in Christ.

Orthodox believe these mysteries are not just symbols in the modern sense of that word. They *are* what they symbolize, and God uses them to transform us so we can be like Him. John says in his first letter, "Beloved, now we are children of God; and it has not yet been revealed what we shall be, but we know that when He is revealed, we shall be like Him, for we shall see Him as He is" (1 John 3:2). Similarly, Peter writes, "His divine power has given to us all things that *pertain* to life and godliness, through the knowledge of Him who called us by glory and virtue, by which have been given to us exceedingly great and precious promises, that through these you may be partakers of the divine nature. . ." (2 Peter 1:3–4). Orthodox call this process *theosis*. In some way we can't fully understand, by grace we will share in the very life of the Holy Trinity.

Infant baptism was difficult for me to accept at first, but the evidence of scripture and the fathers convinced me. In three places the Book of Acts (10:2; 16:34; 18:8) speaks of entire households becoming Christians, which would include the children. Irenaeus, at the beginning of the second century, writes, "For he came to save all by means of himself—all, I say, who by him are born again to God—infants, children, adolescents, young men, and old men."

When I introduced this idea to our house churches, it stirred up quite a controversy; even my son Tom couldn't accept it at first. Once he'd figured out where our teaching about baptism was going, he stood up and said, "I want you to know, when you start baptizing babies, that's when I get off the train." As it turned out, Tom's daughter was the first infant I baptized. We found the evidence for infant baptism to be that strong.

The last couple of hurdles were the highest: the Orthodox use of icons and the doctrines concerning Mary.

If you've ever been in an Orthodox church, you know the walls are usually covered with paintings of Christ, Mary, and the saints. At the front of the church is a screen with even more pictures, and there are icons on stands. People stand and pray in front of the icons. Some bow and kiss the icons as well, typically making the sign of the cross to show their loving respect for the persons portrayed in the icon. The Orthodox word for loving respect is "veneration."

For me and for the other five men in our leadership group, this looked like a deal-breaker. We'd all come from churches that abhorred the use of images. After all, didn't the second commandment say, "You shall not make for yourself an idol or a likeness of anything in heaven above, or in the earth beneath, or in the waters under the earth. You shall not bow down to them or serve them" (Ex. 20:4–5)?

As we studied the fathers, we discovered a short work by St. John of Damascus, *On the Divine Images*. In our rejection of images we hadn't taken into account the Incarnation. God had taken on our humanity in all its fleshly reality. In Jesus, God revealed himself in matter. Now it was possible for matter—paint and wood—to be windows into the heavenly kingdom, aids to our prayers that bring us closer to Christ, the saints, and the angels they depict. But it wasn't until we began to use icons in our worship services that we really understood: They are a phenomenal reminder that we worship God in the presence of the saints and heavenly hosts. As for the idea of worshiping the paintings themselves, I no more confuse an icon with what it pictures than I mistake the pictures in my wallet for my loved ones.

If I thought there was a danger of worshiping icons, the danger of worshiping Mary seemed even greater. As a Baptist I'd been taught that Catholics prayed to her as if she were a member of the Godhead. If anything, Orthodox Christians honored her even more extravagantly. But in my study of Scripture, I'd come across verses that seemed to give Mary a special place: When the pregnant Mary visits her cousin Elizabeth, Elizabeth says, "But why *is* this *granted* to me, that the mother of my Lord should come to me?" (Luke 1:43). And in the song she sings at the end of her visit, Mary says, "For behold, henceforth all generations will call me blessed." This seemed to set Mary apart from other women. And that made sense, because from the moment of His conception, the baby in Mary's womb was God—God the Son, the Second Person of the Holy Trinity.

In 431, the Council of Ephesus decreed that Mary is rightly called *Theotokos* or "Godbearer." By virtue of her intimate relationship with God the Son, she is all-holy. She is our model for the Christian virtues. And she has experienced *theosis*, the participation in God's very being that, through the grace of God, we all hope to achieve. Along the way we learned that Orthodox venerate Mary and other saints, but we *worship* only God. Understanding the difference between veneration and worship was a great step forward toward Orthodoxy.

AS THE END OF THE 1970S APPROACHED, through prayer and study our group of six had come to the conviction that Orthodoxy taught the pure faith and preserved the traditions and practices of the ancient church. But we were in a quandary: how could we be truly Orthodox? Our problem was solved in a way only God could have devised.

Back when Jack Sparks headed the Christian World Liberation Front in Berkeley, a young man named John Bartke joined a CWLF study group. John later became Orthodox, and after he graduated from college he entered St. Vladimir's Seminary, the seminary of the Orthodox Church in America (OCA). But John remained on the CWLF mailing list. By 1976 he could see the CWLF becoming more Orthodox, and he wrote to Jack in Berkeley.

Jack sent him some of the preliminary papers we'd been discussing but asked John to keep the papers confidential. However, John was so impressed by them that he shared them with Fr. Alexander Schmemann, the dean of the seminary and one of the great Orthodox theologians of the twentieth century. Fr. Alexander called Bishop Dmitri (Royster), the OCA bishop of the Diocese of the South, who had been raised as a Southern Baptist. Bishop Dmitri called Fr. Ted Wojcik, the pastor of St. Innocent Orthodox Church in Los Angeles, and asked him to visit our academy, which was seventy-five miles north in Santa Barbara. Fr. Ted attended a class Jack Sparks was teaching on the Arian controversy and liked what he heard.

Later our California men went to Holy Week services at Fr. Ted's church. They suffered from a severe case of culture shock! The incense, the chanting, the vestments, the icons, the length of the services were all very different from what they were used to. Yet they still believed we were on the right track.

We later invited Bishop (later Archbishop) Dmitri to our Goleta meeting in 1978. He acted as a link between us and the sometimes confusing world of Orthodoxy that seemed to be pulling us toward it. He helped us tremendously in our efforts to understand Orthodox church life and liturgy and to refine and sharpen our knowledge of Orthodox doctrine. But most important was the joy of having a wise and saintly man give us his counsel.

Things now started to move rapidly. Several of us went to St. Vladimir's Seminary and met with Fr. Alexander Schmemann and the presiding bishop of the OCA, Metropolitan Theodosius. (In the Orthodox Church, a metropolitan presides over other bishops of a national church or jurisdiction.)

Members of the St. Vladimir's faculty also came to the academy periodically. Fr. Alexander in particular became a pivotal figure in our journey. He was with us in Santa Barbara in 1978, when we clarified our understanding of some of the key issues that separated East and West. We agreed that Orthodoxy's conciliar model of decision-making went all the way back to the Council of Jerusalem in AD 50, described in Acts 15:6–21. It was James, the Bishop of Jerusalem (and not Peter), who announced the ruling that Gentile Christians did not have to be circumcised. Secondly, the church fathers had spoken of five especially important churches: Rome, Constantinople, Jerusalem, Alexandria, and Antioch. Rome was the first among five equals, but at no time did the fathers acknowledge the later claims Rome made to rule over all the churches.

Also, we learned that Rome arrogated power to itself and slowly drew away from the Eastern churches. Eventually it departed from the Nicene faith by inserting the *filioque* ("and the Son") into the portion of the creed defining the procession of the Holy Spirit. In the East, the original doctrine was preserved: the Father alone is the source of the Holy Spirit's being. In the West, both the Father and the Son are said to be the source of the Holy Spirit. Not only was this a departure from the conciliar creed, it resulted in decreased attention to the Personhood of the Holy Spirit in both theology and devotion.

In 1054, the separation between Rome and Orthodoxy became final when the pope's legates brought a proclamation to Constantinople claiming to excommunicate the city's patriarch. The hostility of the West was confirmed in blood when Constantinople was sacked during the Fourth Crusade in 1204.

From our discussions, Fr. Alexander could see that we were Orthodox doctrinally but not liturgically, so he told us to build an altar and put up some icons. When he got home, he told his wife, "They're Orthodox, but they don't know it yet." It wasn't very long before we did.

The clergy of the EOC in the late 1980s, with the leaders (bishops) in the front row. Left to right: Jack Sparks, Jon Braun, Ken Berven, Peter Gillquist, Gordon Walker, Richard Ballew.

CHAPTER 8

The EOC

BY 1979, WE REALIZED that the NCAO was too loosely united to move together on the road we had to follow into Orthodoxy. Peter, Jack, Jon, Ken, Dick, and I had a leadership role, but that role was informal. Whatever authority we had didn't come from an office we held; it was personal. Like the leaders of the house churches, we were pastors. No one was formally authorized to see that all the churches believed and worshiped in the same way. In the ancient church, bishops had that authority.

I decided we needed a more cohesive structure than a fellowship of churches could provide; we had to unite them. We'd form a church—a new denomination. The six of us would be its first bishops, each responsible for a regional group of house churches. Peter, the youngest, with his outgoing personality and administrative skills, would be our presiding bishop and have general oversight of the church. Even when we agreed this was the path to take, we still had a big problem to overcome. We knew that in the Orthodox Church, as in the ancient church, only those who were already bishops could pass on that office to others. We also knew that no Orthodox bishop would be willing to consecrate us.

In February, 1979, we met in Montecito, California, with the leaders of the house churches. Ninety-five of them attended. We had prepared well: Jack Sparks and Dick Ballew had sent out digests of the material they'd found from Scripture and the church fathers. At the meeting the six of us explained why we needed bishops: We needed to be more than a collection of churches. We needed to profess one faith, celebrate one liturgy, and speak with one voice.

But the problem remained: we had no bishop to consecrate us. After a lot of thinking and praying, we got a copy of the *Book of Common Prayer*, the Episcopal church's prayer book. It contained consecration prayers that seemed to be traditional. So we knelt around a coffee table in the living room of the house where we were staying, and each of us put his hands on the head of the man in front of him and recited those prayers. Of course, we had no authority to do any such thing. It was what Orthodoxy calls uncanonical: a violation of the sacred canons (church laws) solemnly established by the councils. We thought that in our situation we had no alternative. We relied on the Holy Spirit to make up for any deficiencies in what we were doing.

At the next session of the conference, Peter told the men we'd consecrated ourselves as bishops. And he told them God had put it in his heart that we should be called the Evangelical Orthodox Church. There was a resounding "Amen" from the audience. I thought it was the perfect name. We weren't repudiating our Evangelical heritage on our way to Orthodoxy. I had the same devotion to Christ, love for the Bible, and commitment to sharing the truth I'd had before. Only now those things found a place within Orthodoxy.

Then Peter announced that we would consecrate additional bishops to preside over the house churches in each city, because without the strong leadership bishops could provide, our church would never hold together. We consecrated twenty more bishops at the conference.

Not everyone at the meeting agreed with this. One man, an airplane pilot who was a stalwart in one of my Nashville churches, called a cab and left Montecito before the meeting was over. Another leader said simply, "It's not for me," and though he remained a friend, he never came with us to Orthodoxy.

The formation of the EOC was widely covered by both the secular and Christian press. The idea of a church that was both Evangelical and Orthodox was difficult for them to understand, a puzzling mixture of two diametrically opposed ways of being Christian.

When we told Bishop Dmitri what we had done, we were anxious about how he'd react. "Well, men, to tell you the truth," he admitted, "what you've done is quite uncanonical, but I'm glad you've done it. Up to now, nobody's been in charge, and at least now there's somebody we can dialogue with." That was the beginning of our official discussions with Orthodoxy. An Orthodox bishop or some other representative of Orthodoxy attended every leadership meeting we had after that.

The meeting was a happy one for me. We had solved our organizational problems, and with our new authority we could step up the pace of introducing Orthodoxy to our people. We could also move ahead in our quest to find a place for ourselves in the Orthodox world. At the same time, I was still wounded by the loss of Ray Nethery's affiliation and grieving over the

Ohio churches that would be leaving with him. It was hard to say goodbye to so many people we'd worked, prayed, and worshiped with over so many years. I knew they'd never return.

ONCE THE EOC WAS ESTABLISHED, we began to introduce more Orthodox elements into our worship. Perhaps the most important step we took was to standardize our liturgy. In order to do that, all our bishops, not just the six of us, had to agree, and that led to some fairly stormy debates. How would we introduce more elaborate liturgical worship to our house churches? It would be new and more than a little strange. And what was that liturgy supposed to be like?

We'd been using the basic format Justin Martyr described in the second century—a service of the Word, with scripture readings and prayers, followed by the Eucharist, with an offering of gifts of bread and wine, prayer to consecrate the gifts, and then communion. But Justin only gave an outline. Our Orthodox friends told us if we were going to be truly Orthodox, we'd have to fill it in. Ironically, even though I was the one who had resisted liturgical worship the most, Jack Sparks and I were the ones assigned to work it out. We decided we should use the Liturgy of St. John Chrysostom, the same liturgy used in the Orthodox churches.

St. John Chrysostom was the archbishop of Constantinople at the end of the fourth and beginning of the fifth century. Because of his outstanding preaching he was called Chrysostom, which means "golden-mouthed." The liturgy that comes down to us from him and its traditional ceremonies can seem overwhelming to a Western Christian. The service is entirely sung to exotic-sounding melodies; the clergy wear silk and cloth-of-gold vestments; prayers of intercession for the church, the nation, and the people are repeated frequently; icons are everywhere in the church; the sweet smell of incense, liberally used in the liturgy, permeates the church building; the congregation often bows and makes the sign of the cross.

In order to help our people adapt to the liturgy, Jack and one of our other men set the hymns of the liturgy to familiar Protestant melodies. The heavenly host must have been amused to hear a hymn praising the Theotokos (Mary the Mother of God) sung to the tune of "Rock of Ages"!

Slowly, bit by bit, we became more and more Orthodox. We ordained our pastors as priests and began to refer to them as "Father," and we ordained other dependable men to assist them as deacons. We began to wear black shirts and clerical collars. We taught more about Mary, the councils, the sacraments, and the icons. We introduced vestments. We began to use incense. In Nashville, my friends and I mounted icons on portable screens and took them with us from church to church for the liturgy.

All these changes, of course, didn't come without a cost. We were asking a lot of our people. To move into Orthodoxy, they had to overcome the prejudices many of them were raised with and adopt a vastly different style of worshiping, praying, and, with Orthodoxy's many fasts, living. Even some of our most faithful church members were upset. People I had pastored for years, dear friends of ours, were confused and unsettled. I did my best to help them make the transition. But I knew it wasn't my efforts that would keep people with us; it was the work of the Holy Spirit.

For example, our friend Kathy McCollum had been raised as a Roman Catholic, then became an Evangelical at Ohio State. Eventually her parents and their whole family followed her. To them, it seemed that Kathy was reverting to the religion they'd left behind in their search for the truth. Confused, they asked her, "Why are you going back? Aren't the Bible and your relationship with Jesus enough?" Kathy struggled with their opposition and her own doubts until she truly thought she couldn't come with us. After much prayer, she finally boiled it all down to one question: What is the right thing to do? The answer she received was, "Keep going down this road."

Others, even among the house church leaders, couldn't accept it. Our Belle Meade friends who'd stayed on through the NCAO fell away when it was clear we were becoming Orthodox. Though some of them have remained our friends, it was sad for me to see others, including some who'd been close to us, drift away. Their going left an empty place in my heart.

Sometimes I felt as unsettled as my people did. Not about Orthodoxy; I had no doubts about that. The faithfulness of so many and the progress we were making in introducing Orthodoxy made me feel as if I were on the top of Mt. Everest. However, parting from friends made me feel as if I were at the bottom of the Marianas Trench.

In the end, all our problems proved to be simply growing pains. Almost all the Nashville house churches that came with us into the EOC grew into strong and vibrant communities. People were drawn to them, and many became members of the church. The same thing was happening in other areas of the country too.

MEANWHILE, THE ACADEMY IN GOLETA was training our clergy and leaders in Orthodoxy. I went out to California every so often to spend a week teaching at the academy. Then the six senior bishops decided we should all be together in Goleta to teach and to talk things out among ourselves. I should say that five of us decided. I wasn't interested in teaching full-time. Mary Sue and I were settled in our log house, and I loved my work in Nashville. I didn't want it to wither away while I was gone; who could I trust to keep it going and enlarge it? At the same time I worried that I'd grow away from the other five men if I wasn't with them. And all of them felt we needed to meet more often if we wanted to keep the church from fragmenting. So as a matter of obedience, I agreed to go.

We chose another man to substitute for me in Nashville. I had my doubts, but Fr. Peter and Fr. Jon trusted him. I wasn't happy about leaving at all, but reluctantly Mary Sue and I packed up and went to Goleta. The church had bought us a house across the street from Fr. Peter's, and I began teaching theology and evangelism to the academy's students.

Fr. Jack Sparks was the official leader of the academy. He and Fr. Richard Ballew collaborated on numerous academic papers and pamphlets that refined our understanding of Orthodox teaching and practice. Fr. Jon Braun was still the charismatic preacher he'd been in Campus Crusade, and his high energy drove our meetings forward. We respected his scholarship—he had spent a great deal of time studying on his own, and he and I were the only ones with seminary degrees. Fr. Ken Berven continued to direct our publishing projects, and Fr. Peter Gillquist coordinated all our work. I taught several classes and continued to test our doctrinal findings against the Holy Scriptures. With input from our local clergy, we formalized our teaching in written papers referred to as "The Institute of Biblical Theology (IBT)," used by local parishes for training their members in Orthodox theology and practice.

Topics included in the IBT began with a thorough exposition of the Book of Romans, Paul's most detailed discussion of the church. Then we covered church history, soteriology (the theology of salvation), the teachings of the church fathers, the seven ecumenical councils (including the statements of belief produced by each council), and the major heresies that have plagued the church. We developed twelve extremely detailed catechism lessons, complete with a teacher's outline and a student's outline. Our members were repeatedly exposed to this material and were expected to be well-informed on each topic.

We offered weekend teaching sessions called the Weekend Institute of Biblical Theology (WIBT). Usually an experienced priest would travel to a new mission or to a location that wanted more intense teaching. He would cover ten hours of teaching from Friday evening through Sunday afternoon. This happened typically twice a year. Our people loved these training sessions so they could catch up with the doctrine they had missed in their prior religious teaching.

Classes at the academy were over by noon, so we had plenty of time for study and discussion. Two or three times a week we'd gather on the patio at Fr. Jack Sparks' house. Some of the men would light up cigars, and we all would talk about the progress and issues in our churches. Those meetings were the reason the men wanted me in California. It would have been impossible to exchange ideas so freely and have that level of coordination at a long distance. Those experiences of shared worship, prayer, and study helped me grow in my understanding of the Christian life. I was grateful for all those things.

I WAS STILL OFFICIALLY the bishop of Nashville and began to receive troubling news from home. The difficulties were confirmed by my occasional visits and longer stays in the summer, when classes at the academy were over. Things got so bad that it became apparent that if I didn't go back and take charge, my churches would be destroyed. I couldn't let that happen. I'd worked hard—very hard—to build them up, and they were too important to the members and to the group effort to allow them to just disappear. The other five men pleaded with me to stay in Goleta, but nothing they said could dissuade me. I knew I belonged back in Nashville.

When I arrived home, I uncovered problem after problem. All house churches have difficulties. In such small groups people see each other's foibles, and personality clashes and differences of opinion are magnified. But now, to make matters worse, nearly everyone had been wounded by the unpredictability of the man who had been my substitute. People were at each other's throats. There was loud groaning and bitter complaining everywhere I turned. Some people just up and left. My replacement failed to deal with the discord, and his erratic behavior made the atmosphere even more negative. Many, thank God, remained faithful, including every single man I had ordained. I grieved, wondering how I was going to put the pieces back together.

The first thing was to ask my substitute to leave. Most of our biggest problems stemmed from him. I discovered he was an alcoholic, which explained his instability. The men back in California eventually came to agree with me that he should leave. Despite his experience in Nashville, the man still wanted to be a leader in the church. He went on to two other cities, and, sadly, got into more trouble and was asked to leave both.

Healing the wounds he left was a long, slow process. It took five years for things to settle down, but the bitterness lingered. I was still hearing the same stories and the same complaints. "Lord," I prayed, "will there ever be a time when I won't have to hear about all that?" The Lord took another five years to answer my prayer, but after ten long years harmony returned.

AFTER MARY SUE AND I SETTLED back at Grace Valley Farm and I'd dealt with the most pressing problems, we expanded our work. In our living room we began classes for new members and inquirers, using materials prepared by Frs. Jon Braun, Dick Ballew, and Jack Sparks. Some nights we managed to squeeze as many as fifty people in there!

Meanwhile, Fr. Alexander Schmemann continued to teach us, coming to Nashville twice for conferences (in addition to his visits to our West Coast churches). During his second visit, in 1981, he came to dinner at our home. Although he was the leading theologian in American Orthodoxy and the outstanding figure in the OCA, Fr. Alexander had no pretensions. His only goal was to help us into Orthodoxy.

Both his personality and his writings had a tremendous impact on me. I began to read his books: *Water and the Spirit, For the Life of the World*, and *Introduction to Liturgical Theology*. I was teaching at the academy when I finished reading the *Introduction*, and I told Fr. Jack Sparks, "Somebody needs to write an introduction to his *Introduction*, because it's written on such a high level that reading it is a struggle!" But for me these books were life-giving. They helped me see deeper into the wisdom of Orthodox spirituality, the power of the liturgy, and the strength of its theology, all presented in a way a Westerner could understand.

One day I told Fr. Alexander I was struggling to be bishop over seven house churches. "I've been teaching the Bible to our people for several years, with three weekly study groups. I spend a lot of time preparing for them. Then there are the home church meetings, with the Eucharist at each location on Sunday following our common meeting for the Liturgy of the Word." Up to that time we typically met early on Sunday morning for the Liturgy of the Word in whatever space we could find. We met in the Hall Electric Company's upper floor, the Admiral Benbow Inn, a hall in the Nashville Civic Center, and a YMCA. We finally found the Harris-Hillman School and were able to meet there for several years, but initially continued receiving the Eucharist at the individual house churches.

Fr. Alexander thought for a moment. "Let me give you a suggestion," he replied. "Why don't you consolidate the seven churches into one for the Eucharist? You can continue going to the house churches for Bible teaching and fellowship, but have the Eucharist together on Sunday morning."

Fr. Alexander's suggestion was just what I needed. I was so weary of trying to keep the house churches going that I put his plan into action quickly. We obtained a three-panel icon painted by Jan Isham, four feet high and twelve feet wide, to serve as a backdrop for the altar area. It depicted Jesus Christ, surrounded by angels and the twelve apostles, blessing the world and offering the Eucharist in a chalice. Soon we began to conduct the Liturgy of the Eucharist in the school's gymnasium immediately after the Liturgy of the Word. That was a major improvement, but we still had to perform a great deal of work each Sunday, putting up the very large icon and other fixtures and then taking them down and removing them after the service. It became obvious that we needed a church building of our own.

Bill and Dottie Hall and the Batsches paid off the remaining mortgage on the farm, and there was plenty of land available, so in 1985 we decided to build there. And it was then that the talents of my good friend Bill Hall came to our assistance.

Bill was an outstanding contractor and an alcoholic who had finally quit drinking after several false starts. He began a Bible study primarily for alcoholics that he nicknamed the DBC— the Drunks' Bible Class—and I proudly led that class for many years whenever I could be available, typically early on Saturday mornings.

Calling in favors from his friends in the construction industry, Bill oversaw the construction of a building that would seat about 150 people, which in later years was expanded to seat over 200— and he and his wife Dottie paid for most of it. Initially dedicated to the Holy Trinity, the church building became an anchor for us. We could worship in a place of our own instead of being nomads in living rooms or rented spaces.

Availability of our own building had fueled our growth, so then Bill led the second stage of our building program. Almost by himself he built a fellowship hall next door to the church that would hold our members for coffee hour and other social events, and the Halls also paid for that. The fellowship hall was built of logs, similar to those used in our home but with siding on the outside. The hall also held Sunday school classes, a small bookstore, and some office space. We finally had facilities suitable for our needs, at least for the next several years.

THE PROBLEMS THAT AROSE during my two years in California weren't our only challenges. None of us who were bishops knew how to do the job. As we began to use our authority, we made quite a few missteps. We emphasized obedience. We instituted a disciplinary system, complete with church courts, and were sometimes overly severe in our judgments. Our people were very close and sometimes tried too hard to solve each other's problems. Our leaders believed God was inspiring them to handle the details of our people's lives, and we were treading on a lot of toes. With help from disgruntled former members, the press started printing critical articles about us. That, combined with our exotic Orthodox ways and theology, led some in Evangelical circles to describe us with the dreaded word *cult*.

Many of the members of our Belle Meade Bible studies attended First Presbyterian Church in Nashville, a very influential church not only among Presbyterians, but in Nashville's wider Christian world. While I was still in California and the house churches were in turmoil, some of our people turned to First Presbyterian for help.

One of the more prominent members of First Presbyterian heard some of these stories and formed a negative opinion of our church. As a young man he had committed himself to Christ and became a staunch Calvinist. He was a deacon in his church and taught a large Sunday school class. He liked to teach about cults and the occult, and one Sunday he taught a class on the Evangelical Orthodox Church. For him, it was just another cult, heretical in its theology—no total depravity of fallen man, no predestination of the non-elect to damnation, no bondage of the will, no irresistible grace, no idea that Christ died only for the elect, no notion that a Christian couldn't turn away from Christ. And then there were the matters of our liturgy, our church discipline, our idol worship, and our ideas about Mary, and if all that weren't enough, we had the gall to call ourselves Evangelical!

When I heard about what this prominent leader was teaching, I was more than upset. He was spreading misinformation—and very damaging misinformation—about our church. I wrote to him immediately and asked if we could meet. I wanted to correct his misconceptions and explain why we were moving to Orthodoxy. I appreciated his importance in the Evangelical community, and I wanted to get to know him and see if he and I could work together on issues and problems in the community where we agreed. When no answer came, I called him directly to see if we could get together. He reluctantly agreed to see me in his office.

After we had exchanged the usual greetings, he launched into a diatribe. He told me—emphatically—everything that was wrong with the EOC. He had quite a list.

Now, I don't often get angry, but when I do, I get *angry*. It seemed as if steam were about to burst out from under my clerical collar. I did the most prudent thing I could think of: I left. "I don't think this meeting is getting us anywhere," I said crisply as I got out of my chair.

"That's fine with me," he snapped. The edge in his voice told me that if I hadn't left on my own, he would have thrown me out. Clearly, my ability to be both Evangelical and Orthodox wasn't easy for others to grasp. When my anger died down, I was left feeling sad that I hadn't been able to get through to him.

To his credit, he and his wife attended a Pascha (Easter) service at our church a few years later. They then returned for additional services, and today he and his wife are both pillars of the parish.

MEANWHILE WE CONTINUED our efforts to find a way for the EOC to be recognized as truly Orthodox. In 1981, one of our priests in the Midwest met a Greek Orthodox priest and discussed our situation with him. The Greek priest told him to contact Bishop (later Metropolitan) Maximos, the Greek Orthodox bishop of Pittsburgh. "Bishop Maximos," the Greek priest told him, "loves converts. He thinks we should be building a truly American Orthodoxy." News of the conversation got to Fr. Peter Gillquist, who made a phone call to Bishop Maximos. The bishop asked Fr. Peter to come to Boston and give a talk to Orthodox college students. Then in 1982, Fr. Peter was invited to meet with the faculty of Holy Cross, the Greek Orthodox seminary in Boston. He was invited back to Holy Cross the next year to lecture on preaching the Bible. Bishop Maximos was with him on both occasions. In between those visits, he met with Archbishop Iakovos, the head of the Greek Orthodox Archdiocese of America (GOA).

In the midst of all this, Fr. Peter asked me to go to a meeting at the Baptist Conference Center in Bagdad, Kentucky. Bishop Maximos was going to meet with a group of Baptist leaders because Baptists had deployed missionaries to evangelize in the northeast. Some of them were working among the Orthodox, trying to convert them away from what the Baptists saw as their false religion and "save" their souls. The Orthodox bishops were very concerned about this and had arranged this meeting to address the problem. Fr. Peter couldn't go, and at the last minute, he asked me to go in his place.

"I'll go if you want me to," I said, "but I'm almost certain there'll be men I went to seminary with at the meeting. And I'm not sure I want to sit in a meeting with them and have to explain why I'm wearing a collar. What's worse, they'll see that I'm claiming to be an Orthodox bishop. I'm worried about how they'll react."

When we got to the meeting, I tried to be as inconspicuous as possible. I sat in the back row, determined not to say anything.

Bishop Maximos presided. "I'd like to introduce," he began— he's soft-spoken, and you can hardly hear him if you're not in the front row—"all the representatives of the Baptist Church who are here. Would you please stand?" They all stood and introduced themselves. It was a high-level group of men, all in leadership positions. I saw two people with whom I'd gone to seminary. One of them was a prominent theologian at Baylor University.

"Well," Bishop Maximos said, "now I'd like to introduce our Orthodox representatives." There weren't as many Orthodox as there were Baptists. "And," he continued, "I'd like to especially welcome Bishop Gordon Walker of the Evangelical Orthodox Church, who's also here with us."

I wanted to crawl under one of the chairs in front of me. *Why did you do this, Bishop?* I thought. One of the men I'd been in seminary with turned around and looked at me. He seemed puzzled, as if he were thinking, *That man looks like someone I knew at seminary, but why would he be wearing a black shirt and a clerical collar?* Later he told me Bishop Maximos was speaking so softly he hadn't been able to catch my name.

I was even more disconcerted when Bishop Maximos said, "Bishop Walker will be speaking to us tomorrow morning." This was a surprise to me, and when I calmed down, I knew I'd have to explain my spiritual transformation to my former colleagues without offending them in the process.

That night I struggled to write a talk. I called Peter. "What am I going to say?" I asked anxiously. "And how am I going to say it?"

"Just tell your story," he replied, "and let the Holy Spirit lead you." I tried to write a speech, but the words wouldn't come.

By the time I managed to put something down, it was ten o'clock. Still worried about my talk, I knocked on Bishop Maximos's door. "Oh, don't worry about it, Bishop," he said reassuringly after I had explained my dilemma. "Whatever you say will be all right."

"Well, here's what I've written so far," I said uncertainly, handing him the manuscript.

I was anxious as I watched him read through it. When he finished, he looked up and nodded. "This is fine," he said. Reassured, I went back to my room and stayed up late into the night finishing the talk.

The next morning was bittersweet. In a sense I was saying goodbye to the church that had formed me and given me so many precious memories. But I was also relieved that I'd been able to give these men an accounting of what I had come to believe and how I had gotten to where I was now. In fact, the talk went so well that we published an expanded version of it as a pamphlet, *Odyssey to Orthodoxy*.

BASED ON THE HELP and encouragement we'd received from Bishop Dmitri and Fr. Alexander, we in the EOC had set our hearts on being taken together into the OCA. In 1985, most of the leaders of our churches, including the core of six, met out in the mountains near Santa Barbara. We were trying to figure out ways to bring all of our churches into canonical Orthodoxy. Then came the blow.

"Men," Bishop Dmitri told us, "several bishops in our synod are adamant. We cannot receive you as a group. Both your lay members and your clergy will have to come into the church individually. If your clergy are to be ordained by us, they will have to study at an Orthodox seminary. They will have no official connection to their EOC brethren."

I was devastated by what I had just heard. For me, acceptance by the Orthodox churches was a necessity. I had to be *truly* Orthodox. I could no longer bear being on the outside looking in. But the OCA proposal was devastating. Our people wouldn't be able to stay together; they'd each have to go to the nearest Orthodox church. That would have destroyed our parishes. I was convinced very few would make the huge leap to a local Greek or Russian or Arab church, feeling skeptical that they would be accepted in what was essentially an ethnic community.

After so much hard work, so much study and prayer, we weren't going to disband our parishes or ask our people to make

such hard choices. If we stayed together, we could help Orthodoxy break out of its ethnic enclaves and offer its treasures of doctrine, liturgy, and spirituality to Americans of every background.
But how on earth were we going to bring a whole denomination
of two thousand people with us?

The original temple of St. Ignatius Church under construction, 1985

CHAPTER 9

Constantinople

DESPITE THE REBUFF WE'D SUFFERED from the OCA, I felt more urgency than ever to become truly Orthodox. No Orthodox church in America was going to recognize the EOC as a sister church, and now it looked as if none would receive us as a group. The longer we remained outside the Orthodox Church, I thought, the greater the chance that our churches—even I myself—would fall away. If we couldn't all go together, I'd have to go by myself.

In January 1985 the bishops of the EOC met to discuss the situation. After a few hours of talking, we ran out of ideas about what to do next. Then an idea occurred to me. *It's a long shot*, I thought, *but we might as well try*. I rose from my chair. "Why don't we go to Constantinople"—now Istanbul—"and talk to the ecumenical patriarch?" I asked. "Surely he can help us find a way to bring our people into Orthodoxy."

In the ancient church there were five patriarchates, one in each major city: Rome, Constantinople, Alexandria, Antioch, and Jerusalem. Since Rome was the capital city of the empire, the patriarch of Rome was "first among equals." He was acknowledged to be the first patriarch in honor, and what he said was carefully listened to, but he had no power or jurisdiction over the others. He was a patriarch, not a universal ruler.

Gradually Rome moved away from Orthodoxy, a movement culminating in its separation from the Orthodox Church in 1054. The patriarch of Constantinople took the place of the patriarch of Rome as first among equals; he is now called the ecumenical patriarch and is recognized as first in honor by all the Orthodox churches. Like his predecessor in ancient times, he has no authority over the other patriarchs. If anyone was in a position to lead us into Orthodoxy, he would be the one.

The men were uncertain about my proposal. "Do you think that's possible?" one of them asked skeptically.

I suppose I was pretty naive that day, but yes, I did believe it was possible. "Let's ask Bishop Maximos about it," I suggested.

After we'd been rejected by the OCA, Bishop Maximos had helped us bind up our wounds. He urged us to continue our quest and became our staunchest advocate. I volunteered to call him. Coincidentally—or perhaps it was more than coincidence—right after I left the meeting I got a message that Bishop Maximos wanted me to call him. He asked me to speak at an ecumenical renewal conference in Pittsburgh.

When I asked him about making a trip to see the patriarch, he was enthusiastic. "Oh, Father, I'll help you to go!" he said. "And not only that, I'll go with you. My spiritual father is on the patriarchal synod in Istanbul. And so, yes, I'll help you do that."

We began planning the trip for that summer. During all this period of happy anticipation, we referred to the city as

Constantinople in recognition of what it had once represented: the home base of the Holy Orthodox Church.

"If we go in early June," Bishop Maximos told us, "we can go to the Pentecost liturgy at the patriarchal cathedral and visit the island of Halki, where I went to seminary. It will be the seventh anniversary of my consecration as a bishop."

Bishop Maximos volunteered to arrange things at the GOA in New York. The ecumenical patriarch presides over the church of Greece and the Greek churches abroad because he is the patriarch of Constantinople, once the capital of the Byzantine Empire; he is the leader of all the Greek Orthodox in the Ottoman Empire. As a courtesy we wanted the American branch of the Greek Church to know what we were doing. Nineteen of our EOC bishops would go to Istanbul; each would bring a gift for the patriarch.

In May, Peter Gillquist and his wife, Marilyn, traveled to New York to celebrate their wedding anniversary. While they were there, they visited the headquarters of the GOA to ask Archbishop Iakovos, its ruling bishop, for his blessing on the trip. They were told he had the flu and couldn't see them. It was disappointing, but they weren't worried; Iakovos had already told Bishop Maximos he could take us to Istanbul.

A few weeks later, we were on our way to Istanbul. On the first leg of the trip, I flew from Nashville to New York to get a flight to London. When we landed at JFK, I went to the international departures lounge to find Bishop Maximos. As I looked around the lounge, I saw a friend, Fr. Gregory Wingenbach, a priest in the GOA. His wife is Greek, so he's tied to the Greek community, and he's been in the GOA for many years. I got to know him when he was pastor of the Greek church in Nashville, and I was surprised to see him at the airport.

Fr. Gregory walked over to me. "Hello, Father," he said.

"What are you doing here, Fr. Gregory?" I asked.

"Oh, well, I'm coming in Bishop Maximos's place."

I had no idea what was going on. "What? What do you mean?"

"There's been a complication, Father, and Bishop Maximos isn't able to go with you. He's sent me in his place."

I was angry and upset about this sudden change of plans, and I struggled to maintain my composure. Fr. Gregory and I were roommates during the trip, and he worked at keeping me calm the whole time. But one thing I knew immediately: We were in for trouble in Istanbul.

In London there was more troubling news. Fr. Peter had to leave a day earlier than the rest of us because of an airline strike. While he was in the air on his way to London, a telegram was delivered to his house: YOU MAY NOT GO TO ISTANBUL, it read. CANCEL YOUR TRIP IMMEDIATELY. It was signed IAKOVOS. What did it mean?

In Istanbul, we were told that an itinerary had been set for us by church officials. We couldn't understand why everything had been prearranged, and we still didn't know why Bishop Maximos hadn't been permitted to go with us.

ON PENTECOST SUNDAY we went to the patriarchal cathedral for the liturgy. I was heartened to see how many people were there. We'd heard that few people still participated actively in church life because, faced with hostility from the Turkish government, the Greek community in Istanbul is small and shrinking.

But right before communion, almost everyone got up and left the church. I heard buses starting their engines outside and came to the horrifying realization that those people hadn't been there to worship with us at all; coming to the service was just part of their sightseeing tour. The only people left in the church now were a tiny group of locals . . . and us. When it was time for communion, I didn't see a single person go up to receive. *This is Pentecost Sunday*, I thought, *not all that far from Pascha* [Easter]. *Why isn't anybody taking the Eucharist here?* Whether it was indifference, fear of communing unworthily, or a lack of preparation, I was shocked. Regular communion was so much a part of our life back home that I couldn't imagine a liturgy with no one receiving the Lord's Body and Blood.

After the liturgy was over there was a brief break, and then the kneeling service began. The kneeling service marks the end of the fifty-day Easter season, when no kneeling is allowed. We'd never been to this service before. The kneeling service contains long prayers by St. Basil the Great during which everyone kneels and makes prostrations, stretching out and touching their foreheads to the floor. This service was all in Greek. Fr. Gregory had warned us we'd be kneeling on the hard stone floor (most Orthodox churches don't have pews or kneelers) for a long time. Forewarned or not, my knees were not happy.

At the end of the service the patriarch got up and served us the *antidoron*, bread that has been blessed but not consecrated. I expected one of the clergymen to invite us to meet the patriarch. But instead, the patriarch and his entourage, all the members of his synod, marched out of the church and left us there. I turned to Fr. Gregory and asked, "Where are they going?"

"Oh," he said, "the service is over. Everything is finished. We'll have to go out now and get taxis and go back to our hotel."

"What?" I exploded. "We spent fifty thousand dollars to bring twenty-odd men all the way over here. We collected three thousand dollars to give to an orphanage of the patriarch's choosing. We've brought gifts from every single parish in our church; we have suitcase after suitcase of stuff to give him. And we're not even going to see him?" I'm afraid I was not all that Christian about it. "You go find somebody to come back here and talk to us," I demanded.

"Okay, okay," Fr. Gregory said unenthusiastically.

He went up to the patriarch's party and stopped them just as they reached the church door. After some back-and-forth in Greek between Fr. Gregory and the patriarch's attendants, two men came back to where we were standing. One was an older man, Metropolitan Maximos, the spiritual father of our dear friend Bishop Maximos, who'd been unable to come with us. The other was Metropolitan Bartholomew, who later himself became ecumenical patriarch.

With a mixture of kindliness and curtness, they explained, "We're sorry, but you can't visit the patriarch. He is very busy, and there have been some complications. We hope you enjoy your pilgrimage here in the Holy City of Constantinople." And then they left.

We were stunned, angry, and hurt. We left the church to find a bus waiting for us. I was puzzled. "I thought we were going to take taxis," I said. Without asking us, someone had chartered a bus and arranged a tour for us; they wanted to take us on a boat ride to the Bosphorus.

Every one of us was furious as we got on the bus. Harold Dun-away, who founded our church in Alaska, was particularly angry. I admired Harold, but I was also a little afraid of him. He'd been in the military, and when he was upset, his language showed it. He gave us a colorful display that afternoon.

The rest of us didn't explode as spectacularly, but we were distraught. "What on earth have we done this for? We've wasted our time. We've wasted our money. We're not interested in going on a boat ride on the Bosphorus."

The man in charge of the tour bus tried to calm us. "Listen, this has all been arranged as part of your travel package. You've already paid for it."

"Look, we may have paid for this," someone snapped, "but if we don't want to go, we don't want to go. Why should we when we can't even talk to the patriarch? That's what we came over here for."

"You've *got* to go on this boat ride. You're in the Middle East," the tour leader explained, "and when you make an agreement like this here, it's a great insult to the people who arranged it if you refuse to go." So we stayed on the bus.

During the ride we found out that the tour guide was a secret agent, not for the KGB or the CIA, but for Campus Crusade. He was quietly working in Istanbul to evangelize the Turks. "*Please* go on this boat ride," he pleaded. So we did. It was an interesting experience. Many of the ships we passed were Soviet oil tankers and aircraft carriers sailing the Bosphorus from the Black Sea to the Aegean.

The trip gave us time to let off some steam. It began to rain, and most of the men stayed on the upper deck, which was covered with a canopy. Dick Ballew and I went down to the lower deck; he paced one way and I paced the other. We were both perplexed and asked each other, "What have we managed to do so far? Why are we here? Does God have any purpose at all in bringing us here?"

After we got back to the hotel, we went to the hotel bar. I sat next to the chairman of the classics department at the University of California at Santa Barbara, who was with us as our interpreter. Mary Sue and I had lived next door to him while I was teaching at the academy, and we had developed a close friendship.

As we were chatting, he said, "You know, I've known most of the members of the patriarch's synod for years. I served with them in various capacities when I was in Greece. Maybe I can talk to them." I was doubtful that he could accomplish anything, but word of his offer spread through the group. We agreed the best plan was for him to write a letter to the synod explaining how important it was for us to meet with somebody from the patriarchate. We'd brought money, we'd brought gifts. Wasn't it possible to meet with a member of the synod, even if we couldn't meet with the patriarch himself? The professor offered to hand-deliver the letter.

His assignment proved much more difficult than we anticipated. After the morning liturgy at St. George, the patriarchal church, the synod bishops visit other churches scattered across the city. Istanbul is huge and covers both the Asian and European sides of the Bosphorus. The professor spent a lot of our money on buses and taxis trying to locate these men. But somehow he tracked them down and got them to agree to bring the matter up with the patriarch. It was finally decided that we would visit on Wednesday.

We had to choose a small delegation to represent our group. Naturally, our presiding bishop, Bp. Peter Gillquist, would go. I went as bishop of the eastern archdiocese (all the churches east of the Mississippi), and Bp. Richard Ballew as bishop of the west. We chose two deacons to go with us: Harold Dunaway's son Marc and Col. Tom Webster (who was serving in Santa Barbara). The five of us squeezed ourselves and our suitcases of gifts into a taxi. The presents we brought included three beautiful jars of Mary Sue's blueberry jam and quilts lovingly made by our parishioners in Nashville. There were gifts representing each parish, along with a photo album of all our churches.

We met for forty-five minutes with Metropolitan Bartholomew, who was the secretary of the synod, and Metropolitan Maximos, the spiritual father of my dear friend Bishop Maximos of Pittsburgh. In addition to wanting to help us, the opportunity to see Metropolitan Maximos one last time was another reason Bishop Maximos had agreed to go with us in the first place. "If you have a chance to get to know him when we're in Constantinople," Bishop Maximos had told me, "please do."

The representatives of the patriarchate were polite, but they gave us no instructions about coming into the Orthodox Church and no encouragement in our quest. "Just keep talking to the churches in America," was all Metropolitan Bartholomew would say. It was our only meeting with them. And as it turned out, the Pentecost service was all we would see of the patriarch. He didn't put in an appearance at our meeting.

But one good thing did come out of our conversation. Metropolitan Maximos was the only man the Turkish government allowed to live at the former patriarchal seminary on Halki Island in the Aegean Sea, an hour's boat ride south from the great city, now just plain old Istanbul. He invited us to come to Halki the next day with our whole group. He promised to provide us with a meal and show us the seminary and the library.

The visit to the seminary was the high point of our trip to Istanbul. We were allowed to examine second- and third-century manuscripts, the kind that can only be looked at through glass in museums, and to look at them close up. To touch those pages was like touching the hands of the church fathers themselves. It was a deeply spiritual experience.

We saw other profoundly moving things on our trip. We prayed in the few Byzantine churches in Istanbul that hadn't been turned into mosques. We marveled at the magnificent Hagia Sophia, the Church of the Holy Wisdom, built by the emperor Justinian in 537 and now a museum. On our way back home, we stopped in Thessalonica in Greece, where I stood on the stone St. Paul is said to have stood on when he preached the gospel to the Thessalonians. We sang the Trisagion hymn, "Holy God, Holy Mighty, Holy Immortal, have mercy on us," in the oldest surviving Christian church.

WHEN WE GOT BACK TO THE US, we asked Bishop Maximos why he hadn't been able to be with us and why Archbishop Iakovos had forbidden us to go.

"Less than a week before our scheduled departure," the bishop told us, "Archbishop Iakovos summoned me to New York for an urgent meeting. 'You can't go to see the patriarch,' he told me. I was astonished. I tried to protest, but the archbishop was adamant.

"'Why can't I go? What's wrong?' I asked.

"'I'll let someone else answer that,' the archbishop replied, and he called a distinguished-looking man into the room. 'This is the Greek ambassador to the United Nations,' Archbishop Iakovos said sternly. 'The UN isn't in session, but the ambassador has come from Athens to explain to me the Greek government's views on your trip.'

"'We cannot allow you to see the patriarch,' the ambassador said. 'Our relations with the Turkish government are tense, and the Turks are looking for excuses to restrict the patriarch's activities. If he receives a group of Americans, the Turks will wonder what is going on. Besides,' he said, with a nod to Iakovos, 'the Greek Archdiocese is the defender of our Greek culture in the United States. We don't want our parishes taken over by an influx of non-Greeks who don't understand our traditions.'"

Now I understood. We had looked to the ecumenical patriarch to show us a way into Orthodoxy. We had thought, as his title implied, that he was open to the whole world. But he was living in an environment hostile to both his faith and his ethnicity, and his first concern was to shepherd his own flock.

In addition, he presided over the church of Greece and the Greek church in America. And as the ambassador told Bishop Maximos, one of the paramount concerns of the Greek church and the Greek government has always been the preservation of Greek culture in the large Greek-American community. The children and grandchildren of Greek immigrants have been moving into the mainstream culture and away from the old ethnic ways. Given all that, the patriarchate and influential clergy in the Greek Archdiocese had no interest in having a large group of non-Greek converts join their church, whose Orthodoxy they thought was only skin-deep and who might water down their faith as well as their culture. Our road to Orthodoxy wouldn't be by way of Constantinople, or Istanbul as we now called it.

When we were in Thessalonica, we met with the head of the Orthodox seminary there. After listening to our story and our disappointment, he reassured us, "There will be a way for you to get into Orthodoxy."

Yes, Lord, I prayed. *There will be a way. No matter how hopeless things have seemed, you've always seen us through.* I knew that being Orthodox, really Orthodox, was a matter of spiritual life and death for me. I *would* be Orthodox. But where? And how?

CHAPTER 10

Home at Last

B ACK IN APRIL, 1985, while our group was planning the trip
to Constantinople, Fr. John Bartke again stepped forward to
help us in our quest for Orthodoxy. He had already introduced
us to major Orthodox theologians by sending some of our writings to Fr. Alexander Schmemann, who shared them with other
Orthodox leaders. Now he came to tell us that Metropolitan
Philip of the Antiochian Archdiocese and Patriarch Ignatius IV,
Patriarch of Antioch and all the East, would be in Los Angeles shortly after our projected return from Constantinople. He
offered to schedule a meeting with the two great leaders. Even
if he didn't suspect that the trip to Constantinople could fail, he
made one very important point: however we eventually came into
Orthodoxy, we would want to know the senior hierarchs in each
jurisdiction. The meeting was scheduled for late June, 1985, in
Los Angeles.

As Fr. Peter, Fr. Jon Braun, and Fr. Richard Ballew traveled
to the meeting, they managed to shake off their depression. They
explained to both hierarchs why we wanted to become Orthodox
and summarized all the studying we had done for over fourteen

years to prepare for entry into Orthodoxy. The two hierarchs were remarkably cordial, and speaking together in Arabic, they agreed they must try to help us enter Orthodoxy. If not, they felt they would never be able to face the Lord on judgment day.

A schedule was quickly established for transmitting massive amounts of information about the EOC to the metropolitan's headquarters/residence in Englewood, New Jersey, and planning future meetings. Both sides worked hard at this process, and by early September, 1986, an agreement in principle had been reached for the EOC to enter the Antiochian Archdiocese.

Everything did seem in order for a swift, final "yes" vote on the issues. Yet when we met at the metropolitan's headquarters in Englewood on September 5, 1986, some of his counselors were still recommending that he go slowly and put off a decision, even offering this advice aloud in the meeting. Their words seemed like a wet blanket thrown over the metropolitan's initial enthusiasm.

Finally, I could not stand the suspense or the fear of another rejection, nor could I control my emotions. Weeping aloud, I said, "Brothers, we have been knocking on Orthodox doors for ten years, but to no avail." And then to the Metropolitan I said, "Now we have come to your doorstep, seeking the Holy Catholic and Apostolic Faith. If you do not accept us, where do we go from here?"

He remained thoughtful for a few moments, then threw open his arms and said, "Welcome home, brothers." But he also advised us to study one more time all the documents that had been drawn up and decide if we unanimously wished to enter Orthodoxy via the Antiochian Archdiocese.

He later stated that my outburst confirmed his belief in our sincerity and strengthened his determination to see that we were taken into Orthodoxy. When I first brought Mary Sue to the archdiocese to meet him, Metropolitan Philip again emphasized that my outburst had not offended him; he even showed Mary Sue the chair I had been sitting in at the time.

Five days after this first meeting, we went by his office again with our fifteen bishops and fifteen observers to confirm our acceptance of all the details of the coming transition. Fr. Peter had already told the metropolitan by phone that our answer was "yes." We therefore expected to say a few brief words and then be gone, but Metropolitan Philip came to the door personally to greet us. He insisted we come in, and we found that a great feast had been prepared for all of us. As we stared at the elaborate spread, he again threw open his arms and exclaimed, "Welcome home, brothers!"

The joyous celebration ended with brandy and cigars on the patio. Usually I don't smoke, but that day I made an exception. Metropolitan Philip has since said that he knew from the beginning of this final series of meetings that these sincere seekers should and would be accepted into canonical Orthodoxy, and he never doubted his decision to be the one to accept us.

When I saw Metropolitan Philip's outspread arms and heard his "Welcome home!" I felt the touch of the Holy Spirit. My eyes were full of tears, but they were tears of joy. After all the years of searching, after all the doors that wouldn't open, we were home. I was home. Home at last.

As we celebrated the EOC Divine Liturgy on the Saturday before our acceptance, we were observed by the metropolitan and some of the clergy he had appointed to advise us. I was a little anxious about their reaction. They suggested we make some changes, but I was relieved that on the whole they were satisfied with our liturgical practice. The next day we attended the Antiochian liturgy at the metropolitan's church, yearning for the day when, as Orthodox Christians, we could receive communion with our Antiochian brothers. Now it would not be long in coming.

Before we left Englewood, we discussed the details of how we would be received into the Antiochian Archdiocese. All our members had studied Orthodoxy in detail and had already been baptized in the name of the Father, Son, and Holy Spirit, so to enter the Orthodox Church we would only need to be chrismated. (Chrismation, the anointing of a person with chrism—oil mixed with spices—accompanied by many prayers, corresponds to confirmation in the Western church. Chrismation confers the Holy Spirit on the subject and is usually administered as part of the baptismal liturgy.)

Metropolitan Philip thought the clergy who had been leading our house churches were well educated in Orthodoxy, and he decided to ordain them without requiring any additional theological training. Our EOC deacons would be ordained as Orthodox deacons and our priests as Orthodox priests. However, in the Orthodox Church bishops must be unmarried, so those of us who were EOC bishops would be ordained as priests. As a group, we would have our own identity: what had been the Evangelical Orthodox Church would become the Antiochian Evangelical Orthodox Mission, charged with the task of sharing our joy in Orthodoxy with other American Christians.

The news of what we were doing hit Nashville like a

bombshell. Many people we'd known in the Evangelical community shook their heads in disbelief. They'd thought we were eccentric, to say the least, but now it seemed we were tossing our Evangelicalism aside to join an idolatrous foreign church. And not everyone in the EOC was overjoyed either. Despite the care we had taken to prepare our people for the fullness of Orthodoxy, some were shocked that we were actually taking the final step. Just as at the previous crossroads in our journey, there were those who couldn't follow us. In the end, almost a quarter of our membership nationwide chose not to go into Orthodoxy, and to my sorrow, friendships and family ties were once again strained and sometimes broken.

There was plenty for me to do when I got back to Franklin. Forms had to be filled out and sent to Englewood for each parishioner who would be chrismated. I had to complete paperwork for each EOC priest and deacon who would be ordained to serve in our Nashville church. In addition, we had two men who were ready for ordination, and I had to ordain them prior to the time of our reception into the Antiochian Archdiocese. I'm glad I did: Fr. Stephen Rogers succeeded me as senior pastor and is an excellent priest, and Fr. Bob Sanford serves the parish faithfully as well as assisting smaller parishes. There were other EOC parishes in the vicinity that would be sending their people and clergy to Franklin to be chrismated and ordained; I had to make arrangements for them too.

Then there was the matter of what to call our church in Franklin. Our parish was dedicated to the Holy Trinity, but there was already a Greek church in Nashville with that name. I'd been thinking about naming the church after St. Athanasius, but

Metropolitan Philip sent us a list of three names, and St. Athanasius wasn't on it. St. Ignatius of Antioch was.

Throughout my pilgrimage, St. Ignatius had been both an inspiration and a light beckoning me forward. Back in the days when I was walking up and down the dusty path in front of our log house editing Fr. Jack Sparks' translation of the Apostolic Fathers, I was especially moved by the letters of Ignatius. He was one of the earliest witnesses to the orders of ministry in the church, and his writings taught me that it had always had bishops, priests, and deacons. He clearly and forthrightly taught the true presence of Christ in the mystery of the Holy Eucharist. He had preached Christ fearlessly and then sealed his testimony with martyrdom. I hoped his prayers would help our church to be faithful and grow, to be a sign of Orthodoxy in an environment that knew little of it. We would name our church after St. Ignatius.

OUT IN CALIFORNIA, Metropolitan Philip chrismated our West Coast members and ordained Fr. Peter Gillquist, Fr. Jack Sparks, Fr. Jon Braun, Fr. Richard Ballew, and Fr. Ken Berven to the Orthodox priesthood. Next he would come to Franklin to chrismate and ordain our people and clergy. I think one of the reasons he came to Tennessee himself rather than sending Bishop Antoun, who was traveling to other EOC parishes to perform chrismations and ordinations, was that he wanted to see our little church sitting in the middle of the Evangelical heartland. On February 17, 1987, our church building was filled to overflowing when Metropolitan Philip came to receive us into Orthodoxy.

A few weeks before the service, I asked Metropolitan Philip

if Bishop Maximos of Pittsburgh, one of our guides through our journey to Orthodoxy, could be my godfather. He had been so kind and helpful to me and to all of us in so many ways that I wanted to have a special spiritual tie to him. I didn't know what the proper protocol among bishops was, and I was afraid that I'd offend Metropolitan Philip. He laughed kindly and said, "Sure. Write him and see if he would like you to be his godson." I did, and Bishop Maximos was happy to claim me.

In the church that day, candles flickered in front of the icons placed on stands for veneration or hung on the wall. The smoke of incense hung in the air, and the church was filled with the sound of chanting. Metropolitan Philip stood in front of our simple icon screen wearing richly embroidered vestments. Barefoot, my heart beating with anticipation, I approached him. Dipping a small brush into a vial of Holy Chrism, he anointed my forehead, chest, lips, ears, eyelids, hands, and feet, saying at each anointing, "The seal of the gift of the Holy Spirit." All of me—mind, emotions, senses, my power to work and to walk in the path of holiness—was now prepared to serve God and come to participate in His nature.

Many times in my life I have felt the presence of the Holy Spirit, from the day when, as a small boy, I walked the aisle of the Pinson Baptist Church to give my heart to Christ. Now the Holy Spirit was filling me with power as never before. Here I was, at the end of a long, winding, wearying, and sometimes discouraging road, finally at the place where God had intended me to be all along. My heart was full as Metropolitan Philip prayed, "Thou art justified. Thou art illumined. Thou art sanctified; in the Name of our Lord Jesus Christ, and by the Spirit of our God."

The day after the chrismations we were ordained as deacons. Then the day after that, those of us who had been priests and bishops in the EOC were ordained as Orthodox priests. On both ordination days, the church was again filled with our newly Orthodox parishioners and friends gathered to support us in our new ministry by their presence and their prayers.

The day I was ordained a priest remains one of the most important days in my life. After the Great Entrance in the Divine Liturgy, when the bread and wine for consecration are brought to the altar, I knelt before the Metropolitan with my hands on the altar. He laid his hands on my head and prayed the prayer of consecration of a new priest: "The divine grace, which always heals that which is infirm and completes that which is lacking, ordains the most devout Deacon Gordon to the office of Priest. Let us, therefore, pray for him, that the grace of the All-Holy Spirit may come upon him."

As meaningful as my previous ordinations had been, I knew—I could feel—that this was different from my Baptist ordination or from that night around the coffee table when my five friends and I consecrated each other as bishops. Metropolitan Philip stood in an unbroken line of bishops that went back two thousand years to the apostles of Jesus. With the touch of his hand he made me a priest, a successor of the presbyters of the New Testament. This, at last, was the end of a long but meaningful journey.

METROPOLITAN PHILIP had to take a lot of criticism from others in the Orthodox hierarchy for what he did for us, but he had done his homework. In deciding to perform multiple chrismations and ordinations during a single service for the EOC members entering the Antiochian Archdiocese, Metropolitan Philip searched the Scriptures, the practice of multiple Orthodox jurisdictions over the centuries, and the canons of both local and ecumenical councils.

The Scriptures reveal abundant evidence, in both the Old and New Testaments, of multiple individuals being received at the same time by anointing with oil and/or the laying on of hands. All jurisdictions continued with multiple chrismations/ordinations until recent centuries, and the Patriarchate of Alexandria continues the practice to this day. The metropolitan could find no canons from any source either condemning this practice or limiting the number of acceptances on a single day, nor has a single critic produced such a canon. If a canon forbidding cluster acceptances had been valid at one time, Metropolitan Philip could have waived it under the principle of *ekonomia* (economy), a flexible interpretation of the usual practices in order to carry out the church's primary mission, to bring people to Christ. But it was not necessary to invoke *ekonomia;* he simply followed the Scriptures and the church's ancient practice.

It is correct that the custom of multiple chrismations/ordinations has decreased in use in recent generations, but not because of any official restrictions. It can be truthfully stated that Metropolitan Philip enthusiastically restored the ancient scriptural and early church practice of multiple chrismations/ordinations during a single service. While a few officials complained, he and his new Orthodox believers rejoiced again and again.

Years later, Metropolitan Philip said, "Words are inadequate to describe the joy which permeated my heart when I was chrismating and ordaining these wonderful people. Before this, I used to chrismate little Middle Eastern children with dark hair, brown eyes, and olive skin, and suddenly I found myself chrismating little blond, blue-eyed and fair-skinned children. . . . After the reception of these beautiful people into canonical Orthodoxy, I was criticized severely by some frozen-minded Orthodox. I didn't care. And if I had the opportunity to do it again, I would shout a million times, 'Welcome home, brothers!'"

Fr. Peter Gillquist and Fr. Gordon, 2009

CHAPTER 11

Being Orthodox

IN MANY WAYS THERE WAS LITTLE DIFFERENCE between pastoring outside the Orthodox Church and pastoring within. I still used the tools I had learned as a Baptist: personally visiting members and prospects, preaching from the Bible, and teaching small group Bible studies. To those I added activities I learned in the EOC: celebrating the Divine Liturgy, hearing confessions, and administering the other mysteries.

But there was one big difference between now and then. Now I was doing those things with the authority of the church through the ages. I wasn't ministering according to my own interpretation of Scripture or some historical construction I had built in my mind. I was following the model that had been established by Jesus Christ Himself and transmitted over the course of two thousand years to me. I felt an assurance of my ministry that I had never really experienced before.

As had always been the case in ministry, I found many new members through Bible studies. Romans was still my favorite book in the Scriptures; but because of its complexity, teaching it was demanding for both my students and me. So I usually started with one of Paul's less difficult letters, like Philemon. I would teach for about an hour and then take questions from listeners.

At a series of studies we held at my son Tom's house in nearby Murfreesboro, I managed to go through almost all of Paul's epistles verse by verse. I tried to deal with people where they were, both spiritually and in their knowledge of Scripture. It pleased me to see how engaged with the Scriptures they became. I wasn't trying to convert them; I wanted to strengthen them to live a Christian life and grow closer to God. But converts did come, as they always had from my Bible studies. Eventually (after two years) there were more than twenty-five families, enough to establish an Orthodox mission, now St. Elizabeth Antiochian Orthodox Church.

To me one of the tragedies of modern life is that people do not take time for regular, intense Bible study. By the same token, priests must find the time to conduct Bible teaching on a regular basis. As clergy and laypeople work together, faith and commitment grow in the individual and group, often resulting in outcomes such as the beginning of St. Elizabeth's.

Bible studies weren't our only source of converts, however. Our parishioners brought friends and relatives to experience our services. People who were looking for something more than their Protestant churches could provide came to inquire, and in many cases stayed. And sometimes our big log house has played an important role in helping people make decisions.

We've had all kinds of people come to our log house to sit in front of our fireplace or stay for a while in one of our spare rooms. Some have been Orthodox looking to grow in our faith or to talk over problems. Many have been seekers looking for a spiritual home, and often they have found it. Our house has been a sanctuary for Protestant ministers who need space and time to transition to Orthodoxy. It's even been called a station in the underground railway to the Orthodox Church. I think anyone who has the blessing of being Orthodox should be ready to gently and patiently share their faith with others, often finding that a personal growth in faith has occurred from the process.

Our log house has been especially useful in helping Orthodox believers come to the decision to pursue a Christian vocation. St. Ignatius has produced four priests, four monastics, and a number of deacons, a commentary on the spiritual strength of our people. A number of those came to that commitment after living in our home for the length of time required to answer God's call.

One particular group of young Antiochian seminarians from the late 1980s comes to mind. Rick Michaels, Alan Shanbour, and Pat Kinder started working with children at Antiochian Village, a camp and conference complex founded by Metropolitan Philip. While singing for the children they developed a repertoire of Orthodox-themed folk music that was way outside the Antiochian tradition. In the 1990s their music became popular with Orthodox young people, and soon their group Kerygma (Greek for "proclaim") was giving concerts all over the country.

When they came to Nashville to record their first CD, the three of them stayed at our log house. They ended up spending two years in Nashville, off and on, as guests in our parish, usually staying in our log house, sometimes in a house in Nashville that belonged to the parish. Alan is now Fr. Michael, Pat is Fr. Patrick, and Rick, ordained Fr. Anthony, was consecrated a bishop on December 11, 2012. He now serves as the Antiochian Bishop of Toledo and the Midwest.

WHEN I WAS TEACHING Bible classes at Ohio State, I began graduate studies there and enjoyed the challenge. After I was feeling settled into Orthodoxy, I decided to complete my studies and earn a doctorate. I found a program that allowed me to study on my own and attend classes once a month. So once every month I headed north to the campus of Notre Dame in South Bend, Indiana, where our classes were held.

It was quite a different experience for me. I enjoyed studying even though the courses were taught from the liberal point of view and many of the things we studied were way outside my comfort zone. But after years of reading the Scriptures, I was immune to the liberal view of the Bible. I wasn't intimidated by my teachers, and I managed to hold my own in what could have been a very hostile environment. I spoke up when I thought something needed to be challenged, but I tried hard not to be hostile or obnoxious in my questioning.

Despite my disagreements I was awarded a doctoral degree. One day I was discussing it with a fellow priest who was eager to sign up for the program. Then he asked me a question that seemed to come from left field: "Did you have any trouble getting your bishop's permission?"

Permission? It never occurred to me that I needed the bishop's permission. I still had a lot to learn about the ins and outs of Orthodox church life.

It may not have been an instance of the old adage, "It's easier to get approval after the fact than it is to get permission," but when I told Metropolitan Philip what I had done, he was more pleased than annoyed. In fact, he thought continuing education for clergy was a fine idea and started setting up regular study programs for priests.

MEANWHILE, OUR FORMER EOC PEOPLE were being more closely integrated into the Antiochian Archdiocese. We always followed the directions of our bishops, making sure that our liturgies followed Antiochian customs and that our music was the same as that used in other Antiochian churches: no more guitars or "Rock of Ages" tunes! We were anxious to do as much as we could to fit in and not to think of ourselves as special. We were still students and realized that our teachers knew a lot more than we did.

As our parishes were becoming more active participants in their respective dioceses, our separate identity as the Antiochian Evangelical Orthodox Mission became less and less important. When the AEOM was finally disbanded, Fr. Peter became head of the Department of Missions and Evangelism of the archdiocese. We six—Fr. Peter Gillquist, Fr. Jon Braun, Fr. Jack Sparks, Fr. Richard Ballew, Fr. Ken Berven, and I—continued our regular meetings for a time.

Initially we still published our magazine *Again*, but eventually it became too expensive to publish a slick, four-color magazine, especially since the archdiocese also publishes a similar monthly magazine, *The Word*.

Conciliar Press went on publishing books and has steadily grown; it is now Ancient Faith Publishing and offers a full line of gifts and devotional items, along with its own publications and selected Orthodox books from other publishers. It also has a sister organization, Ancient Faith Radio, which offers podcasts and other online broadcasts of Orthodox material. Together they form Ancient Faith Ministries.

The academy moved to Sacramento, where the cost of living was lower than it was in Santa Barbara. Fr. Jack Sparks became less and less involved in it as time passed due to his declining health.

Our major collective contribution to the church after we were received into the archdiocese was a publishing venture that began separately from what was then still Conciliar Press. Shortly after we were chrismated and ordained, the six of us met together and talked about Bibles. For more than a century, study Bibles have been popular with Protestants. When I was a Baptist, I used the *Scofield Reference Bible*, first published in 1909. Now there is a bewildering array of study Bibles available covering every imaginable age and interest group. Catholics have study Bibles as well, but there were no Orthodox study Bibles. We agreed that was exactly what was needed to give seekers and converts an Orthodox perspective on Scripture and to invite cradle Orthodox to deepen their understanding.

Fr. Peter, our organizer, and Fr. Jack, our researcher, took charge of the project. We were blessed to have Metropolitan Maximos as one of our general editors. Our overview committee included some of the most prominent scholars in the Orthodox world as well as eight metropolitans and four archbishops, among whom were the ruling hierarchs of the largest Orthodox jurisdictions in the US.

Fr. Jack distributed the work among the members of the

academy and the various scholars who were part of the project. I was assigned the commentary on the Book of Sirach (also called Ecclesiasticus), one of the Old Testament books of the Greek Bible—the Bible of the first Christians—that Protestants don't use because it isn't in the Hebrew canon. It wasn't a text I'd read in my Baptist days, even at seminary, so I had a lot of catching up to do. I worked on the study notes in odd moments when I was traveling. It took all of three years to finish them.

For the New Testament we used an existing Bible translation, the New King James Version, which was based on the same Greek manuscripts we Orthodox use. But for the Old Testament it was necessary to prepare a new English translation of the Septuagint, the Greek version of the Old Testament in common use during New Testament times and the version quoted by Jesus Himself.

We feared there might be little interest and sales might not break even with costs, but Thomas Nelson Publishers took the chance anyway. It is gratifying that sales have far exceeded expectations, and that the *Orthodox Study Bible* remains the most authoritative and most popular study Bible among Orthodox Christians. We are happy to have had a role in producing this treasure for Orthodox Christians and for all others who wish to know more about the truths of Christianity.

WHILE ATTENDING A CONFERENCE in the early 1990s I met a young priest, Fr. Daniel Byantoro. Fr. Daniel was a real rarity, an Indonesian Orthodox priest. Indonesia is a Muslim country; ten percent of the population is Christian, and most of those belong to the Dutch Reformed Church, which was planted there when

Indonesia was a Dutch colony. Fr. Daniel told me one of the most amazing stories I have ever heard.

Fr. Daniel was born into a Muslim family and, encouraged by his grandfather, was a staunch defender of Islam during his high school years. One day while reading the Qur'an he saw a bright light, and he recognized Jesus in that light. At first he was frightened, but then his fear gave way to great joy. *Who is this Jesus Christ?* he asked himself. *What does he have to do with me?* He then flipped through his Qur'an and stumbled on chapter 3, verse 45: "Remember when the angels said: O Maryam [Mary], surely Allah gives you glad tidings with a Word from Himself, His Name will be the Messiah, Isa [Jesus], the Son of Maryam. He is great in this world and hereafter, and he is among those who are near to Allah." After much more study as to the meaning of the term "word," Daniel became a Christian convert from his own reading of the Qur'an.

Fr. Daniel first joined a charismatic Evangelical Protestant group and then attended seminary in South Korea. While there he encountered Orthodoxy and soon recognized it as the true New Testament church. He was chrismated and ultimately ordained as that rare entity, an Orthodox priest who was a former Muslim. He was soon accepted by the Indonesian government as the leader of the Orthodox Church in Indonesia.

Recognizing his obvious talent and his commitment to Orthodoxy, I began to help him with contributions from Grace Ministries to his seriously underfunded work. Soon we formed Friends of Indonesia, an organization devoted to supporting his ministry, and a number of faithful supporters began to donate to that organization regularly. We also formed a group known as 500

Founders, dedicated to raising funds to support the building of a missions center for his work. Each contributor to that cause is recognized as a founder of the Orthodox witness in Indonesia.

It is not easy being a Christian in a Muslim country, and it is even more difficult to be an Orthodox priest in a country in which the government colludes with Muslim officials in the persecution of the church. For example, the government has been known to allow initial permits to begin construction of a building but then refuse to grant permits to allow the work to be completed. A church or monastery therefore stands partially finished to deteriorate from exposure to the elements, purely because of the reluctance of Islamic leaders to allow Christian activity.

Fr. Daniel, a faithful servant of God and of His church, continues his work in spite of resistance from many sources. In recent years the leadership of Friends of Indonesia has passed to others with my blessing, but it remains a worthy cause and one that deserves the support of Orthodox Christians who wish to support mission work in other countries.

IN 1995 I WAS INVITED TO ATTEND the elevation of a friend to the office of bishop at a ceremony to be held in Damascus, Syria. The investiture took place during a marvelous liturgy at the cathedral in Damascus, packed with faithful Orthodox Christians. One thing I noticed was that many of the people sang, and sang beautifully, during that service. Of course we take congregational singing for granted at St. Ignatius, largely because so many of our members are converts from Protestant churches where they have been accustomed to singing, and because we have always encouraged such participation. Sadly that is not the case in many other Orthodox churches, where there is little to no congregational singing.

I took the opportunity of that journey to plan an extended trip to Taiwan and then to Indonesia and Australia to visit Fr. Daniel and other Orthodox leaders in those areas. In Taiwan I brought Orthodox literature, almost impossible to obtain in that country, encouraged the formation of missions and parishes, and counseled people drawn to Orthodoxy. To me this was a mission trip, not a tourist excursion. I did not know it at the time, but this mission trip was the prelude to a great deal of traveling I would be doing beginning the very next year on behalf of Orthodox missions.

While in Taiwan I was introduced to a Protestant missionary named Brian Short by Timothy Beach, a young American convert to Orthodoxy who was in Taiwan to teach English. Timothy had already told Brian of our 1987 chrismations and had described Orthodoxy and his own reasons for conversion; he had also given Brian some literature, including copies of *Again* and *Word* magazines. Brian was intrigued with Orthodoxy, so after several conversations I left him with additional literature, including a service book, prayer books, and a copy of Fr. Peter's book *Becoming Orthodox*, and with an invitation to visit upon his return to the States.

After a lengthy period of self-study and visits to Antiochian parishes in the States, Brian and his family decided Orthodoxy was right for them. Brian is now an active member of St. Ignatius and a board member of Grace Ministries. One of his five daughters is now an Orthodox nun, and another has recently married an Antiochian seminarian. How often I have observed that merely exposing mature Christians to Orthodoxy leads to their conversion to Orthodoxy over time.

I then arrived in Indonesia just at the outbreak of anti-Christian riots. Fr. Daniel carefully hid me, with my white hair and beard, blue eyes, and the cross I wear daily, so that rioters would not discover me, a visiting infidel priest. On this trip and on a subsequent trip to Indonesia I learned the very serious risk of going out in public in the garb of a Christian priest in a volatile Muslim culture. But I was also privileged to see the courage and dedication of young priests who work with Fr. Daniel to preach Christ in a hostile environment.

In Australia I met Seraphim Scheidler, an Orthodox Christian in the ROCOR (Russian Orthodox Church Outside Russia) tradition. He later came to Franklin with his wife Margaret and two lovely daughters; they lived with us for a time while getting established in the US. Because Margaret is a physical therapist and the US has a shortage of physical therapists, she could stay and work here, and her family could stay as well. He and his family were enthusiastic supporters of St. Ignatius. Like many others who have stayed with us, this family benefited from exposure to our Orthodox community, and we in turn benefited from exposure to these gracious people from another culture. After they returned to Australia he was ordained as a ROCOR priest. They then returned to Franklin, where Fr. Seraphim died a few years later. He is buried in an Orthodox monastery cemetery in West Virginia.

AFTER I HAD SPENT NINE YEARS following our chrismation as pastor of St. Ignatius, I got a call from Fr. Peter. "Gordon," he said, "I'd like you to think about working full-time in the missions department. We need you to help new or struggling congregations survive and grow."

Fr. Peter knew I wouldn't say no. I'd answered his call to join him at Campus Crusade all those many years ago, and we had traveled a long road together. Of the six friends who had taken that road, he was the closest to me. He knew I still had a heart for missionary work.

I talked things over with Metropolitan Philip. He told me he also wanted me in the missions department and asked me to nominate a successor as pastor of St. Ignatius. After much thought and prayer, I recommended Fr. Stephen Rogers. He faithfully pastored St. Ignatius from February, 1996, until his retirement in 2017.

As a member of the Department of Missions and Evangelism, I was given responsibility for all our missions east of the Mississippi. I did much of my work by letter and telephone from our log house. Priests and laity who wanted to start missions called me to coordinate their efforts with the archdiocese. Bishops would send me the names of mission congregations that needed help and encouragement. When necessary I went out on the road, typically about twice a month, traveling to small missions to help them resolve their problems and to serve the liturgy and administer the sacraments where there was no resident priest. The work reminded me of my first experience as a pastor, making a circuit of small churches in southern Alabama.

My work with missions is typified by the story of the first mission I went to help, St. Michael the Archangel in Cotuit, Massachusetts, out on Cape Cod. Despite our pastor's attempts to strengthen the mission, it was struggling to attract people, and its financial state was dire. Bishop Antoun talked to me about it, stating that it would likely be necessary to close it because of its poor growth and sad financial state.

I went to Massachusetts weekly and visited every Orthodox believer and every inquirer who had shown interest, not to pressure them, but just to invite them to services and to let them know that we were not planning to close the mission. I conducted Bible studies when possible and held to a set time for liturgy. Many of those who came liked what they saw, and the mission began to grow. It was a joyful experience. I still have many good friends there, and St. Michael the Archangel is now a self-sustaining church.

The same can be said of St. Basil the Great in Poquoson, Virginia, near Williamsburg, which has grown from five to thirty-six families, and of St. Barnabas Mission in Columbus, Ohio, the site of my Campus Crusade years, where five families began and there are now about one hundred members. These small missions have overcome their problems and are now self-sustaining, as are other small missions.

The same techniques described above work again and again: (1) show interest in and visit everyone who has shown any interest in the mission or who is known to be Orthodox or to have inquired about Orthodoxy; (2) conduct small Bible studies; and (3) conduct liturgies on a set basis so that people know what to expect. In working with these and other missions, I often benefited from the help of Fr. Nicholas Sorensen of All Saints Antiochian Church in Raleigh, North Carolina. As dean of the Southeastern Deanery, he has been especially generous with his time and talents in helping these small parishes.

The experience of Ss. Peter and Paul mission in Boone, North Carolina, a mission I started in 1998 which is now a church, demonstrates that laypersons can sustain a mission even when there is no permanent priest. Boone is a resort town in the North Carolina mountains where vacant land is both scarce and expensive, as are empty buildings suitable for use as a church. There are no ethnic Orthodox within the general area. Appalachian State University brings new students to town each year, but few are Orthodox. The parish has hired two priests over the years, but their tenure was brief. Yet the congregation holds readers' services and also celebrates the Divine Liturgy with the aid of retired priests who come when they can. The congregation continues slowly growing, sustained by the efforts of a number of committed laypersons, all of whom hope that just the right priest will be found in the near future. (Ed. note: Ss. Peter and Paul Church has enjoyed more rapid growth in the last few years and has recently purchased land on the outskirts of Boone on which to build a new church.)

In addition to my work with missions, I was given locum tenens assignments occasionally to help established parishes resolve conflicts and get back on the right track. While these projects were never enjoyable on the front end, they were often rewarding once the problems were resolved.

ALTHOUGH FR. STEPHEN was initially reluctant to accept the post of senior pastor, he has worked diligently and successfully in that position. His homilies are especially inspiring, as are the beauty and dignity of our worship. We continue to receive new members and applicants for the inquirers class.

Recognizing that our growth required an update of our physical facilities, Fr. Stephen has led a building program that included lengthening the original church structure (1998), completing a much-needed new parish hall and then removing the outdated old one (2007), and designing and building our beautiful new Byzantine sanctuary (2013–2014). Our growth could have supported a larger structure, but county building regulations restricted us to a maximum of 336 seats. With the recent completion of the beautiful iconography (by the same artist who painted the iconography in Vladimir Putin's chapel in Moscow), the sanctuary is now finished. We often have standing room only on Sunday mornings, and we continue to grow. Indeed, St. Ignatius is now one of the largest congregations within the Antiochian Archdiocese. How pleasing it is to see the faith of our spiritual children in action.

It is gratifying that St. Ignatius has a full program of Orthodox services, including the ministry of Fr. Stephen, Fr. Bob, and our deacons in the altar and of the chanters, choir, and ushers; the work of our many teachers; and the beautiful singing and praying of our people. It is especially heartwarming to see that almost all members receive communion on a regular basis. It is equally rewarding to note that the sense of fellowship and friendship remains strong within the congregation once they leave the service. I see the same care for one another and enjoyment of each other's company that characterized our people when we were a much smaller group. I pray that this commitment to our worship and this sense of conviviality and friendship within the Lord's service will continue to characterize St. Ignatius until the Lord Himself returns.

FOLLOWING MY RETIREMENT from the Department of Missions and Evangelism in 2002, I have maintained a low level of activity at St. Ignatius. I assist with communion almost every Sunday, hear confessions, and counsel those who think I may be of assistance with their problems. We continue to see a steady stream of friends, both old and new, who stop by for a visit and occasionally to stay for a few days. At first I traveled to other parishes to serve as guest priest or to help iron out difficulties, but those activities have all but stopped. For several years both Fr. Peter Gillquist and I continued to serve on the board of Orthodox Christian Laity, an Orthodox support group dear to my heart that has championed Orthodox unity throughout its existence, and I am glad to see their work continue under other leadership. How pleasing it is to witness the continued growth of the Orthodox Christian faith in so many ways. May God continue to bless His holy church.

St. Ignatius Church today

CHAPTER 12

A Vision for the Future

DURING THE LATE 1960S AND EARLY 1970S, the churches in America were confronted with deep and disturbing doctrinal changes. It seemed Christianity was becoming the "Doctrine-of-the-Month Club." Orthodoxy does not change its beliefs with every wave of new, politically correct ideas. We have deep, rich theological foundations that will sustain us until Christ returns. In Orthodoxy we honor faithful adherence to the traditions of the ancient church. Though the so-called Reformation resulted in the stripping of the altars in England and the development of many new sects of radical reformers, all this ultimately resulted in a hollow, shallow Christianity. St. Paul said, "Therefore, brethren, stand fast and hold the traditions which you were taught, whether by word or our epistle" (2 Thess. 2:15). He wrote in another epistle, "Now I praise you, brethren, that you remember me in all things and keep the traditions just as I delivered *them* to you" (1 Cor. 11:2).

The radical rejection of apostolic teaching that is accelerating in many of the mainline denominations in America today is the final, bitter fruit of the Renaissance and the casting off of tradition. How comforting Orthodoxy has been to many of us who had despaired of finding a church that has continued to be true to the apostolic traditions through the whole two thousand years of church history!

WHEN I READ THE NEWSPAPER or watch the evening news, I'm overwhelmed by the reports of violence, corruption, child abuse, murder, rampant immorality, and widespread disregard for law and order. The misguided comments of the professional pontificators only make matters worse. All of this makes me cry out, "Oh God, what can we do to save America?" The forces of darkness and evil, and those who would justify them, seem to be incredibly well-organized and well-funded. In times like these, what does the Orthodox Church have to offer America? I believe we have a great deal to offer—the worship, the theology, the carefully preserved apostolic traditions, the unchanging interpretations and understanding of the Scriptures and early patristic texts—but only if we American Orthodox can overcome our divisions.

It is a primary duty of a Christian citizen to love his or her country and to pray for its redemption. Failing to make any effort toward your country's salvation is a grave sin. As St. Herman of Alaska wisely said, "You cannot save what you do not love."

Christ greatly loved His own Jewish nation, but He spoke and acted in such a way as to demonstrate His love for both Jews and Gentiles. His goal was to establish the New Jerusalem, the church, the kingdom of heaven on earth, encompassing all peoples in the love of God. If we become focused only on our own social class, race, or ethnic group, we hinder rather than help to fulfill Christ's Great Commission: "And Jesus came and spoke to them, saying, 'All authority has been given to Me in heaven and on earth. Go therefore and make disciples of all the nations, baptizing them in the name of the Father and of the Son and of the Holy Spirit, teaching them to observe all things that I have commanded you; and lo, I am with you always, *even* to the end of the age. Amen'" (Matt. 28:18–20).

God calls some of us to be foreign missionaries and serve Him outside our own country. I am one of those; I've made mission trips to seven African countries, Europe, the Middle East, the Far East, and Southeast Asia. But after all those trips I came home and sorrowed over my own country.

Orthodoxy has much to offer our country, but our lack of unity and absence of a shared vision of our redemptive role hinder us. There is no way we can calculate the lost opportunities for outreach and evangelism, the duplicated efforts, the competition for the same resources to fund our institutions and organizations. We often refuse to cooperate with one another for fear that our particular brand of Orthodoxy won't be predominant in the public arena.

Many of us Orthodox Christians are guilty of these failings and more, as are almost all religious and secular institutions. But God's holy church isn't just another organization. It should rise above these self-centered motivations and actions. We all know this, and most of us feel ashamed when we realize we have fallen into these errors. But the church's lack of administrative unity and common vision promotes and encourages these failings. Our church was created for unity in love, not for selfishness and factionalism.

In our fallen world, competition can be a good thing. It forces companies to improve their products and services if they want to stay in business. Perhaps the competitiveness among our church bodies and institutions has a positive side, keeping us striving for the perfection the Lord admonished us to keep as our goal: "Therefore you shall be perfect, just as your Father in heaven is perfect" (Matt. 5:48). But we should strive to please God, not to outdo our neighbors. We should help each other toward the goal of perfection, not race to get there first.

IN THE MOST IMPORTANT WAYS, Orthodoxy in America is already unified. We share the same unchanged Nicene Creed and the unchanging faith taught by Holy Scripture, the church fathers, and the seven ecumenical councils. We all worship with three of the most ancient liturgies of the church (those of St. James, St. Basil, and St. John Chrysostom) and observe the same round of feasts and fasts. All of us use icons in our prayer and venerate Mary the Theotokos and all the saints. We Orthodox don't have any ground for arrogance or pride: the truths we find in the church are gifts from God, and we should receive them with humility. But if we're to share these gifts with our fellow countrymen, we need to unify the Orthodox jurisdictions in America.

I'm not asking our Orthodox people to abandon their links to their mother churches. All of us, cradle Orthodox and converts alike, have received our faith from the Greek, Russian, Arab, and Eastern European churches that were planted in America to shepherd their immigrant flocks. We are tied to them with bonds of love and gratitude, and we have the obligation to honor their traditions and help them to flourish. But no mother who loves her children wants to keep them from growing up and realizing their full potential.

I think it's obvious that the Orthodox Church here in America has yet to actualize its potential. In fact, some of us feel that our mother churches have been reluctant to let us develop. They often represent the interests of their own peoples and countries and stand in the way of our growth into a truly indigenous North American Orthodox Church. Sadly, this is a kind of religious colonialism with no accountability, siphoning off resources and stifling initiative. And it actively hinders the local decision-making process that is essential to a dynamic and growing local church.

The people of the non-Orthodox churches in America support thousands of schools, universities, and seminaries, and tens of thousands of foreign missionaries and institutions. We claim Orthodoxy has been on American soil for two hundred years (if we date our history from the geographically limited Russian missions in Alaska). Yet even if we claim a significant presence of only a hundred years, we still stand embarrassed. We have only a handful of small seminaries, which until lately were all struggling for survival. Our missionary endeavor, as wonderful as it is, is very small compared to the needs. We have no universities and very few parochial schools, secondary schools, or colleges. I believe that if the mother churches gave their blessing to an American patriarchate, our outreach would increase significantly, and our efforts to support and care for the mother churches would increase as well.

SO WHAT SHOULD WE DO? We don't have an American patriarch, and it may be a very long time until we do. What should we do in the meantime? I think St. Paul gives us the answer in Ephesians 4 and 5: "I, therefore, the prisoner of the Lord, beseech you to walk worthy of the calling with which you were called" (Eph. 4:1).

First, we must walk in a manner worthy of our calling as Orthodox Christians. This requires us to be humble, not haughty. We are to be longsuffering, putting up with one another in love, "endeavoring to keep the unity of the Spirit in the bond of peace" (Eph. 4:3). "Endeavor" indicates an earnest, continued effort. We should act as if we had an American patriarch working hard at keeping peace among our jurisdictions and parishes. If we follow St. Paul's injunctions, our parishes will cooperate lovingly with one another to support one another to the full extent we are able.

"*There* is one body and one Spirit, just as you were called in one hope of your calling" (Eph. 4:4). We must keep in mind that we are fundamentally one body. Our multiple jurisdictions are secondary; we serve together under the one Holy Spirit. And all of us have "one hope of our calling," the joyful anticipation of better things to come.

"One Lord, one faith, one baptism; one God and Father of all, who is above all, and through all, and in you all" (Eph. 4:5, 6). These things, rather than any administrative arrangements, are the basis of our unity. Our ethnic identity, whatever it might be, can never overshadow that unity.

"But to each one of us grace was given according to the measure of Christ's gift. Therefore He says: 'When He ascended on high, He led captivity captive, and gave gifts to men'" (Eph. 4:7, 8). We all have been given a special measure of grace by Christ Jesus, and we are expected to put that gift to work in the church.

The One who gives these gracious gifts was crucified and buried and descended into Hades to free the captives there. He ascended into glory to present His trophies of grace to the Father before returning to earth in His resurrected body.

Later in this passage, St. Paul discusses the gift of special ministers and ministries "for the equipping of the saints [here he means all true believers] for the work of ministry, for the edifying of the body of Christ, till we all come to the unity of the faith and of the knowledge of the Son of God, to a perfect man, to the measure of the stature of the fullness of Christ" (Eph. 4:12, 13). *The unity of the faith:* that unity is all important to the witness, the function, and the growth of the church.

"That we should no longer be children, tossed to and fro and carried about with every wind of doctrine, by the trickery of men, in the cunning craftiness of deceitful plotting, but, speaking the truth in love, may grow up in all things into Him who is the head—Christ" (Eph. 4:14, 15). As individuals, as parishes, and as national churches, we need to stop being children, but grow up into Christ. Our goal is to reach the full maturity of Christ Himself. We are not to be "blown about by the trickery of men," which seems to have prevented our multitude of jurisdictions from maturing into a national Orthodox Church.

"From whom the whole body, joined and knit together by what every joint supplies, according to the effective working by which every part does its share, causes growth of the body for the edifying of itself in love" (Eph. 4:16). When all our American Orthodox speak with a single voice and work together in harmony, we will grow in holiness, and as a consequence we will grow in numbers.

Let no corrupt word proceed out of your mouth, but what is good for necessary edification, that it may impart grace to the hearers. And do not grieve the Holy Spirit of God, by whom you were sealed for the day of redemption. Let all bitterness, wrath, anger, clamor, and evil speaking be put away from you, with all malice. And be kind to one another, tenderhearted, forgiving one another, even as God in Christ forgave you. Therefore be imitators of God as dear children. And walk in love, as Christ also has loved us and given Himself for us, an offering and a sacrifice to God for a sweet-smelling aroma. (Eph. 4:29—5:2)

St. Paul admonishes us to speak wisely and lovingly, then gives us a solemn warning: "Do not grieve the Holy Spirit of God." In our divisions, are we kind, tenderhearted, and forgiving? Or do our conflicting priorities and our disagreements result in "bitterness, wrath, anger, clamor, and evil-speaking"? In our immaturity, do we "grieve the Holy Spirit"? Do we put barriers between ourselves and the grace of God? If we are doing all in our power to encourage and work toward a unified Orthodox Church in America, I believe we will be pleasing to God. On the other hand, if we are obstructing this process, I fear we may be grieving the Holy Spirit.

If we are unified in the Holy Spirit, we will be willing to give up our turf for the sake of a truly unified Church. But if we lack the humility and love needed to surrender our jurisdictions and submit ourselves to a truly unified body, led by a holy patriarch who loves this country and deeply desires its redemption, then I believe we stand in danger of severe judgment. May God have mercy on us all!

CHAPTER 13

A Final Word

As the seven of us refugees from Campus Crusade met back in the 1970s, I was forced to confront questions that had perplexed me throughout my ministry as well as new ones that were posed by our studies. The going wasn't easy, but one thing I was sure of: I would follow the truth wherever it led me. I had no idea then that it would lead me to Orthodoxy.

Being a part of the Orthodox Church has given me everything I was looking for, everything I had fought for, and the answers to all my questions. Consider the following eight desires I had and how they were answered in Orthodoxy:

1. I wanted to find the New Testament church.

2. I wanted the full truth of the Bible.

3. I wanted a message I could share with people that went deeper than the message I'd learned to preach.

4. I wanted a wider mission field in which to preach that message.

5. I wanted a church that worshiped God "in spirit and truth" (John 4:23).

6. I wanted a church governed the same way the New Testament church, the church of the fathers, was governed.

7. I wanted a church that could give me concrete, powerful ways to grow closer to God.

8. I wanted the assurance that I was being the best pastor I could be.

1. The New Testament Church

And they continued steadfastly in the apostles' doctrine and fellowship, in the breaking of bread, and in prayers. (Acts 2:42)

Ever since I studied the Book of Acts in Xenia, I'd wondered whether the churches I pastored were truly modeled after the New Testament church. My questioning deepened in Campus Crusade, and the same question led me and my six colleagues from Crusade to begin our in-depth studies. For quite a while we thought house churches were the way to model the New Testament church. It was only after reading the fathers that we had to change our minds. And it seemed to us that they were pointing toward Orthodoxy.

2. The Bible in the Church

And so we have the prophetic word confirmed, which you do well to heed as a light that shines in a dark place . . . knowing this first, that no prophecy of Scripture is of any private interpretation. (2 Peter 1:19–20)

My parents and the Baptist churches I was raised in taught me to treasure the Bible and to study it carefully and prayerfully. Throughout my life, I've looked to the Bible as the wellspring of truth, the source of the pure doctrine and practice of the church. But in my own Baptist tradition and in the Evangelical world as a whole, I saw a confusing collection of understandings, often contradictory, of what the Bible teaches. As a ministerial student in college and seminary, I was exposed to the attempts of modern liberal theology to reject the Bible's inerrancy and its authority. I came to understand that each Protestant church holds to a part of biblical truth but ignores or rejects the parts that conflict with its theology. Although I believed, and still believe, that all of the Bible is the product of divine inspiration, the multitude of conflicting interpretations I encountered produced confusion.

Today I read the Bible from within the church's tradition as God means it to be read, focused on Christ and free of contradiction. It is as if the church fathers are reading over our shoulder, helping us to understand the text as they did. In particular, I have spent many hundreds of hours studying the commentaries of St. John Chrysostom; he too followed the style of teaching the Scriptures verse by verse and chapter by chapter. "Philip ran to him, and heard him reading the prophet Isaiah, and said, 'Do you understand what you are reading?' And he said, 'How can I, unless someone guides me?' And he asked Philip to come up and sit with him" (Acts 8:30–31).

One of the great joys of my life has been to share my love of the Bible with others. From the first days of my ministry in Alabama through my years in Ohio in Xenia, at Campus Crusade, and at Grace Haven Farm; in Nashville, and now in Franklin, I've held Bible classes. For me, it's been the best way to ground the faith of Christians and draw the unchurched to the full Christian life. The difference between my Bible classes before and in Orthodoxy has been the knowledge that what I'm teaching now doesn't depend on my own interpretations or those I learned in seminary. I know I'm passing on the insights of those who were closest to the time of Jesus, some of whom were disciples of the disciples of the apostles.

3. A Deeper Message to Share

Grace and peace be multiplied to you in the knowledge of God and of Jesus our Lord, as His divine power has given to us all things that pertain to life and godliness, through the knowledge of Him who called us by glory and virtue, by which have been given to us exceedingly great and precious promises, that through these you may be partakers of the divine nature, having escaped the corruption that is in the world through lust. (2 Peter 1:2–4)

The Orthodox Church emphasizes the doctrine of theosis (deification), the teaching that we may share in the likeness of God (though not in His essence) by living a godly life of faith and obedience following our baptism. We become more like God through His grace and by exposure to His energies. As many Fathers emphasize, we become by grace what He is by nature; the image and likeness of God with which we were created are restored, and we "become children of God" (John 1:12). This is a message seldom emphasized in denominations outside Orthodoxy.

4. The Great Commission

And He said to them, "Go into all the world and preach the gospel to every creature." (Mark 16:15)

Since my first days as a Baptist preacher, evangelism has been close to my heart. Mary Sue and I longed to go to the ripe mission fields of Africa. When we were unable to go, I found a new mission field through Campus Crusade. My days there, bringing young people to Christ and nurturing them in the faith, were some of the best of my life. And I got a chance to manage Crusade's programs in Africa and even to travel there. I would have been happy staying with Crusade, but God was calling me onward.

Sharing my faith is still an important part of my life. In Orthodoxy I've talked to many, both in the Wednesday-night inquirers classes at St. Ignatius and in front of the fireplace in our log house. I've done what I could, both as a member of the Antiochian Archdiocese's mission department and through Grace Ministries, to bring Christ and His church to people in our country and around the world.

5. Worship

"But the hour is coming, and now is, when the true worshipers will worship the Father in spirit and truth; for the Father is seeking such to worship Him." (John 4:23)

Perhaps the greatest sense of fulfillment I've experienced in Orthodoxy has been true and spiritual worship (see John 4:23). I was raised in a non-liturgical church, and nothing in my background pointed me toward liturgical worship. But I've always wanted to worship God in the way He has established, and as I experienced the Orthodox way of worship, I realized that it is truly patterned after the heavenly worship described by John in the Book of Revelation. As Fr. Alexander Schmemann taught us, when we worship we step out of time into eternity and worship at the throne of God in heaven. All too often, I allow the cares and burdens of life to get in the way of true worship; but when I "lay aside all earthly cares," as the Divine Liturgy urges me, and enter into worship with a penitent and grateful heart, then true worship happens.

6. Governing God's Church

To all the saints in Christ Jesus who are in Philippi, with the bishops and deacons: Grace to you and peace from God our Father and the Lord Jesus Christ. (Phil. 1:1–2)

In the studies of the New Testament and the fathers my friends and I pursued after we'd left Campus Crusade, the way the church was governed was an issue we faced early in our inquiries. It became clear to us that there were bishops, priests, and deacons in the ancient church and that the bishop had the responsibility of overseeing the churches in his area, resolving disputes and making sure the faith was rightly taught and practiced. We had tried to establish the role of bishops in the EOC, but we had to rely on our own ideas of how to do it, and it didn't work out as it should have.

The Orthodox churches have been led by bishops for two thousand years, and they've learned how to do it right. I've been grateful for the guidance and help I've received from my bishops, Metropolitan Philip and Bishop Antoun, in pursuing and practicing pure Orthodoxy in my own spiritual life and in pastoring and evangelizing. On many occasions I have said, "I have been a pastor without a bishop and a pastor with a bishop. I would rather have the bishop, even when he tells me 'no.'" It sure beats trying to figure it out myself or trying to learn it from books!

7. Life in the Spirit

*I press on, that I may lay hold of that for which Christ Jesus
has also laid hold of me. Brethren, I do not count myself to have
apprehended; but one thing I do, forgetting those things which
are behind and reaching forward to those things which are ahead,
I press toward the goal for the prize of the upward call of God in
Christ Jesus. (Phil. 3:12–14)*

From that day when I hurried down the aisle of our Baptist
church to give my heart to Christ, I've tried to live close to Him.
I've tried to be a man of prayer, responsive to the promptings of
the Holy Spirit. I've already shared some of the wonderful things
God has done for Mary Sue and me in answer to our prayers.
I treasure those experiences of closeness to God. In Orthodoxy
I've found a path that builds on those experiences, a profound
and truly enriching spirituality. The fathers of the church and the
desert fathers, who left the comforts of life to struggle with the
obstacles to their relationship with God, gave me an inspiring
and at the same time down-to-earth wisdom to guide my own
spiritual life. Today the monks of Mt. Athos are still pursuing
the fathers' path to holiness, an example and an inspiration to
Orthodox everywhere.

In Orthodoxy I have the means to strive to be the best Christian I can be. I have the treasury of prayers in the Divine Liturgy,
the daily round of church prayers, and a personal rule of prayer,
usually determined in consultation with a wise spiritual father.
And I always know I'm not praying alone: I'm praying with
Orthodox all over the world, with the Theotokos and the angels
and saints whose icons are in my prayer corner. I have the discipline of fasting, during special seasons and on most Wednesdays

and Fridays, to help me to grow in obedience and self-control. Most of all, I have the Holy Mysteries, in which Christ Himself feeds me with His body and blood and forgives me the sins I confess to Him through the ministry of His priests.

8. Tending the Flock

> *He said to him the third time, "Simon, son of Jonah, do you love Me?" Peter was grieved because He said to him the third time, "Do you love Me?" And he said to Him, "Lord, You know all things; You know that I love You." Jesus said to him, "Feed My sheep." (John 21:17)*

From my first experiences in college I've loved being a pastor, working with people and helping them to grow in faith. In Leeds, in Ft. Worth, in Ohio, in Nashville, and here in Franklin, I've tried to give as much time as I can to teaching, visiting, and counseling. As an Orthodox priest, I have no more doubts or hesitations about how and where I'm leading people. And I can do more than counsel. I can confidently pronounce God's forgiveness to those who come to confess their sins. And I can draw on the riches of tradition and two millennia of spiritual wisdom in finding and applying medicine for the wounds of the soul.

ORTHODOXY HAS GIVEN SO MUCH to the two thousand of us who entered the Antiochian Archdiocese almost thirty years ago. But I think there were also some things we brought to American Orthodoxy.

A New Emphasis on the Bible

Then Philip opened his mouth, and beginning at this Scripture, preached Jesus to him. (Acts 8:35)

The kind of scriptural preaching we had learned as Evangelicals is very different from the more doctrinal, church-centered preaching usual in Orthodoxy. We haven't replaced the Orthodox style with our own. Instead, I think we've given more emphasis to Scripture while incorporating the more traditional Orthodox way. We've carried on our teaching ministry through Bible studies inside and outside our parishes and provided a valuable resource for individual and group study in *The Orthodox Study Bible*.

Evangelism

Go therefore and make disciples of all the nations, baptizing them in the name of the Father and of the Son and of the Holy Spirit. (Matt. 28:19)

In modern times the Orthodox Church hasn't been noted for its outreach. For centuries, the churches in the Middle East were under the rule of the Ottoman Turks. The Turks made Orthodox hierarchs responsible for their ethnic communities, and the faith became identified with nationality. Under Muslim rule, the church had no opportunity or ability to look outward. The exception was the Russian church, which planted Orthodoxy among the indigenous peoples first of Siberia and then of Alaska, where it has taken root. But in modern times the Russian church came under severe persecution during the Communist era, and outreach became impossible.

As Evangelicals we were used to looking outward, toward those who didn't share our faith. Wherever I've been in my life, bringing others to Christ has always been the center of my work. Metropolitan Philip had the courage and wisdom to look outward when he accepted us into the Antiochian Archdiocese. He showed a like wisdom when he appointed Fr. Peter to head the diocese's mission department. It's been a joy for me to join in the effort to make Metropolitan Philip's vision of an American Orthodoxy into a reality.

Stewardship

Then they faithfully brought in the offerings and tithes. (2 Chr. 31:12)

Metropolitan Philip was delighted that we had brought the practice of tithing with us to the Antiochian Archdiocese. I think tithing brings great blessings. It shows that you recognize God's lordship over all that you have and all that you are. Since I tithed that dime from my dollar all those years ago, I've been a tithe payer. Not only does it bring me blessings and honor the Lord, it gives the church what it needs to flourish and to grow.

Enthusiasm

For I long to see you, that I may impart to you some spiritual gift, so that you may be established—that is, that I may be encouraged together with you by the mutual faith both of you and me. (Rom. 1:11–12)

All Evangelicals are supposed to have personal conversion experiences, a specific moment of accepting Christ. For me, and I think for many, that experience generated a lifelong desire to give everything I had for the strengthening and growth of God's kingdom. I think we Evangelicals have brought that same kind of joyful dedication to Orthodoxy. And of course Orthodoxy isn't just for me. It moves me to do all I can as a priest to build up the body of Christ and help it grow.

OFTEN PEOPLE WHO DON'T HAVE TO STRUGGLE for something take it for granted. There are many cradle Orthodox for whom their religion is only a habit or an expression of their heritage. My friends and I came to Orthodoxy at the end of a long search marked by repeated sacrifices of attractive options. Most of us received offers to start new Bible-based Protestant churches, city-wide Bible studies, and other religious programs more typical of modern American Christianity.

But much as I was led to lay my wooden bullets on the altar as a child, we sacrificed other offers until we found—and were received by—the New Testament church founded by Christ Himself. For us that reward was like coming to an oasis in the desert, not a mirage but a green place where we can drink our fill of life-giving water. Let us continue to share that life-giving water with all who come our way.

Above: Fr. Gordon's grave in the small cemetery at Grace Valley Farm.
Below: Back of headstone with St. Ignatius Church in the background.

Fond Memories

As this book has come together, a great many old friends who benefited from the ministries of Fr. Gordon over many years have written to tell us how he made a difference in their lives. There are far too many of these to record each one completely, but we have chosen several remembrances that are representative of the group. All of these show the love and appreciation this diverse group of people had for the persons and the ministry they encountered at important times in their lives. We offer these stories as a means of underlining what that ministry has meant to so many.

Bp. Anthony (Michaels), Bishop of Toledo and the Midwest, AOCA

The Very Reverend Fr. Gordon Walker was relentless in his commitment to Christ and his love of the Church. His long journey to Orthodoxy was in my view a preparation for the full expression of his own ministry, which began when he was very young. Being called by God, we do not always know the road we will take, as was the case with Fr. Gordon. His was certainly a path with no variation to the right or to the left. It was a straight trajectory mapped out and planned by God his whole life. He took that road without any hesitation, and he found the Holy Orthodox Church and the fullness of his own ministry. When other people doubted the direction he was going, without flinching and without recrimination he kept moving. When people said he couldn't, he smiled and just kept working. He planted blueberry fields so that people could pick fruit, and in a way he was the one to bring fruit for Christ, which came from the good tree of his dedication. He helped me personally before I was ordained into the priesthood, and finally into the episcopacy itself, by setting the example and by being a reference point for us as young people. His message was clear—"if you don't doubt Christ, there is no doubt you will complete your task." When we look back at his personal career in the Church and his legacy, we know that because it was in Christ, it will continue.

Fr. Nicholas Sorensen, senior priest of All Saints Antiochian Orthodox Church in Raleigh, North Carolina, and dean of the Southeast Deanery, and Kh. Barbara Sorensen

While the 752-mile trip from Atlantic, Iowa, to Franklin, Tennessee, to uncover the Orthodox Church was long and arduous with four children in tow, the journey to become Orthodox was even longer and more circuitous. Who could imagine that one would find the most ancient Christian church in the heart of middle Tennessee?

In February of 1988, less than a year from the time that the EOC entered the Antiochian Orthodox Church *en masse*, we took our four children to "come and see" what would compel so many to seek and find. It was a rough trip in so many ways. Fr. Nicholas was then serving a large parish as a Lutheran pastor. Our children, ages twelve, nine, seven, and three, were curious about this trip, and Barbara was totally skeptical. Was it a midlife crisis of faith that brought Fr. Nicholas on this treacherous trip and odd spiritual journey? If so, how could it become the family's journey? Barbara wasn't ready for such a drastic change. The only thing that gave Father's wife any sense of peace was the fact that we knew Gordon Walker, Jon Braun, and Peter Gillquist from our college days in Campus Crusade, and we respected them as spiritual leaders. If they became Orthodox, then there must be some credibility to it.

From the moment we met Fr. Gordon at the church, we felt warmly welcomed. He understood our struggle and compassionately responded. He was so patient, answering our many questions. Our daughter Krysta, age three, who was very shy, instantly took to him, which warmed our hearts. After that weekend visit, we returned in May of 1988 to live in Franklin, leaving behind a secure position, spacious parsonage, and dear friends to seek the pearl of great price.

Under Fr. Gordon's spiritual guidance, our whole family was chrismated in August of 1988. From that point on, Fr. Gordon nurtured us in the faith, serving us the Eucharist, listening to our confessions, praying for us when we strayed, loving us as his own children. When Fr. Nicholas was ordained, Fr. Gordon was by his side. When we were sent by Bishop Antoun to start a mission in Raleigh in 1993, Fr. Gordon encouraged and supported us in so many ways. In fact, he took in our son, Erik, to live with him that year, as it was Erik's senior year and he didn't want to move.

When Fr. Nicholas was elevated to archpriest, Fr. Gordon came to All Saints Orthodox to serve at the hierarchical Divine Liturgy and lay his humble hands on Fr. Nicholas' head once again.

Arriving a day early for the Parish Life Conference in June of 2015, one month before Fr. Gordon's repose, we had the privilege of sitting down with him in his home and reminiscing about the many blessings we had experienced as a direct result of his service and ministry. Along with Mary Sue, we held hands and prayed together, rejoicing in our common faith. We thank God for the precious time we had with our spiritual father just prior to his going home to be with our Lord. He assured us he knew his time on this earth was over, and he was ready to be present with our Lord.

We thank God for every remembrance of him (Phil. 1:3), for his humble giving spirit that lives on in the lives of his many spiritual children. Memory Eternal!

Cynthia Fox, Ss. Peter and Paul Antiochian Orthodox Church, Boone, North Carolina

Fr. Gordon Walker was a godsend to me personally. I am of Greek descent and was born and raised in an Orthodox church in Fayetteville, North Carolina. I had lived in Boone for ten years without an Orthodox church to attend. My two sons were five and three years of age when I heard that an Orthodox mission was just starting in early 1999. The next Sunday I attended a prayer service at the home of Cameron and Julie Thorpe and knew that I had found my church home. Shortly thereafter Fr. Gordon came to celebrate a liturgy at the American Legion Center in Blowing Rock. Fr. Gordon was the most godly man I have ever met. He was always very kind and encouraging. Thereafter, he stayed at my home when he was in Boone and it was always a joy to host him. My husband George has often said that if every priest was like Fr. Gordon, the whole world would be Orthodox. Because of Fr. Gordon, I was able to raise my two sons in the Orthodox Church, and that means more to me than I can ever express!

Myrna Martin, St. Ignatius Antiochian Orthodox Church, Franklin, Tennessee

I came into the US legally from Guatemala in 1970 to work as a nanny for a family in New Orleans, who promptly moved to Nashville. I soon found myself on call 24/7 to serve as cook, maid, nanny, or whatever they needed. I was paid a small amount but never had time off and could not go to school. I was finally able to go to a retreat for one day with the only Hispanic girl I knew, meeting Fr. Gordon for the first time. Because I was late returning home (we got lost) my employer locked me out. I stayed with my friend for one night and called Fr. Gordon for advice.

He took me into their home and drove me to Memphis to visit the immigration service. They allowed me to stay and promised to come for further evaluation, but never did. Fr. Gordon enrolled me in school, helped me get a social security card and a driver's license, and saw that I went to Bible study and worship regularly.

Along the way I met Deacon Ed Martin, and we married in 1977. Together we and our family have followed Fr. Gordon and the EOC into Orthodoxy, and find the Orthodox life enormously rewarding. As Ed puts it, "you can just get your arms around that living tradition of Orthodoxy that goes back to the earliest days." I am grateful for the help of Fr. Gordon, Kh. Mary Sue, and their wonderful family. I have seen many such examples of love and generosity in his ministry.

Mary Exa Walker Crew, sister of Fr. Gordon, Holy Virgin OCA Church, Charlotte, North Carolina

As I was growing up, I followed the progress of my brother Gordon and his wife Mary Sue through the developments described in this book in their search for the true New Testament church. Despite having attended a Baptist college, I knew nothing of ancient church history, and was therefore surprised at their great satisfaction upon finally entering the Orthodox Church. And then my brother Phillip became Orthodox and was happy with that choice. Certainly something was missing in my own Christian life, despite the hours of service and worship I invested in my Protestant church.

I finally attended a Pascha service at a small OCA church nearby. The Pascha service is so dramatic, so moving, so clearly full of spiritual meaning, and the people were so very welcoming, it was breathtaking. I was hooked. I attended catechism and joined that little OCA church, and I too have found my spiritual home. I owe it to Fr. Gordon and Kh. Mary Sue for bringing our family to Orthodoxy. I'm so glad he kept looking for the true New Testament church. I am now at peace and have found what is so special about our faith. May our Lord be praised.

Margaret Hart Prebonick, RN, of Warren, Ohio

I grew up in Cleveland, Ohio, in a home filled with sadness, tension, and constant fighting. I attended a private Catholic girls' school and was so lacking in self-confidence that many of the girls made fun of me. I hated my life as it was and ran away from home at age sixteen. After a week I made it to my sister's home in Galion, Ohio, and their priest, Fr. John Pasqualin, eventually convinced me to return home. Unfortunately, nothing had changed. After one month I was hospitalized for severe depression, and I just wanted to die because I felt worthless and had no hope. After ten weeks Fr. Pasqualin picked me up at the hospital and took me straight to Grace Haven Farm to live with Gordon and Mary Sue Walker. I never knew how he arranged that.

I couldn't believe the beauty of the farm or the welcoming atmosphere of the Walker family and of the girls who lived in their basement. Everybody talked a lot about Jesus, saying things like "Praise the Lord," and talking about the love of God. I had loved my faith as a child but had lost it along the way. I told Gordon I didn't believe in God and didn't plan to, and he said, "That's all right. We're going to love you anyway." That was my first exposure to unconditional love, but I found it hard to accept because I considered myself unlovable.

One night Gordon sat down with me and began to talk about God's love. He read Philippians 4:6–7: "Be anxious for nothing, but in everything by prayer and supplication, with thanksgiving, let your requests be made known to God; and the peace of God, which surpasses all understanding, will guard your hearts and minds through Christ Jesus." That did it. The light was on. The peace of Christ was for me too! No matter how awful I thought I was! That night I asked Jesus to reveal Himself to me, and the peace, warmth, and joy I experienced have never left me, despite difficult trials that came later. I started to learn about unconditional love and about grace, love not deserved but freely given.

It meant a great deal to me to be a part of their daily family life and to finish high school with their daughter Debbie, who was always so kind and helpful to me. I then left the Walker home to start nursing school at Bowling Green State University, but then they moved to Nashville. I was able to transfer to Vanderbilt and lived with them once again in Belle Meade. This was during the time that Gordon and others were studying the ancient church and slowly finding their way to Orthodoxy.

After my graduation in 1976 I took a job at Akron General Hospital and met my future husband Steve at the Holy Family Church in Stowe, Ohio, where he led the youth Bible study. The Walkers gave us their blessing, and Gordon participated in the wedding service. Steve poured the basement floor of their new log house three weeks later, and then we moved across the road from Grace Valley Farm in 1978. Steve worked on the farm, I worked at Williamson Medical Center, and our first three children were born in Franklin and baptized by Fr. Gordon. The Christian fellowship was wonderful, and we participated in the gradual move toward Orthodoxy. As the group progressively adopted Orthodox practice, it was easy for me to address him as "Fr. Gordon," because he functioned as a loving parent.

After ten years we moved back to Ohio to help with family circumstances, and I reconciled with my parents and helped care for them in their later years. Two of our sons have since lived with the Walkers in their big log house. I can never express my gratitude for all of the wonderful things Fr. Gordon and Kh. Mary Sue have done for me and for our family. Thanks be to God for their ministry and their love.

Fr. Bob Sanford, Associate Priest at St. Ignatius Antiochian Orthodox Christian Church, Franklin, Tennessee

During my middle year of divinity school (1975) I faced a crisis when our Hebrew class was instructed to translate a passage from the Hebrew Bible and then to write a commentary on it, our understanding of what the passage meant. Every member of the class had a different opinion as to the meaning. Furthermore, standard commentaries by professional theologians gave an even greater diversity of opinion.

As I worked on the assignment a nagging thought kept rolling through my brain, like a headache that wouldn't go away. To me the Bible was a book of great authority, expressing truth beyond my small ability to understand it. Those numerous opinions could not all be right; what if they were all wrong? What if I was wrong? How could we know where the truth lay?

Later that year I encountered a group of men who spoke at a Bible conference and who were to contribute greatly to my search for the truth. Their names were Gillquist, Walker, Braun, Sparks, Berven, and Ballew. I soon became a regular at Fr. Gordon's Bible study and at the church services each Sunday. I was greatly impressed with his knowledge of the Bible and with his persistent search for eternal Truth. The story of Grace Fellowship Church, NCAO, EOC, and chrismation by Metropolitan Philip is well told in this book and need not be repeated.

As we moved to Christian Orthodoxy over the next decade, the problem of multiple opinions receded and then disappeared entirely. I now realized that the Truth had already been revealed by the work of the Holy Spirit in the life of the church, in the teaching of the apostles and the church fathers who came after them, in the wisdom of the ecumenical councils and especially in the creed, in the lives and writings of the saints, and, yes, in the Scriptures as given and taught in the church. The Truth was not hidden; it had been revealed and freely given. My job was to learn it, take it, and live it. I did not need to discover the Truth as though I were alone with my Bible on a desert island. Jesus said, "I am the Way, the Truth, the Life." I simply needed to become one with His Truth.

That "middle-year crisis" in divinity school was really only a small voice leading me to look for the Truth. Fr. Gordon led me and thousands of others to find the heavenly Truth of Christian Orthodoxy.

DN. SIDNEY ELLIOTT AND HIS WIFE MARY, former members of St. Ignatius, wrote to express thanks for the time they spent at St. Ignatius. Mary also reminded us that Gordon once took in a frightened horse named Christmas that had been abused. Within a month the residents of the farm had taught the horse to love all who approached. Mary comments that Gordon and Mary Sue similarly adopted abused and neglected people and taught them to love and be loved.

AS DESCRIBED IN CHAPTER 4, JOHN VAVROCH was the Lutheran pastor whom Gordon introduced to Sharon, the girl with the fractured leg. Sharon wrote to say that they were married six months later, and lived a life of Christian service within the Lutheran Church for fifty years until John's death in 2015, shortly before Fr. Gordon's death.

FR. GORDON'S MATCHMAKING was successful on at least one other occasion. A young Antiochian Orthodox woman named Nicole had broken off a relationship with a man named Eric because he was Anglican and had no interest in Orthodoxy. After hearing this story, Fr. Gordon invited both to spend a day at an Orthodox monastery. As she tells the story, she helped the nuns while Fr. Gordon spent the day explaining Orthodoxy to Eric. Several months later Eric was chrismated, and a few months thereafter they were married, with Fr. Gordon preaching at their wedding. They and their three children are now happily Orthodox.

STILL OTHER LETTERS TELL of Fr. Gordon's impact on specific events that were of great importance to individuals. Julie wrote to say that she was the first person Fr. Gordon ever baptized when she was a young girl in one of the rural churches he pastored in southern Alabama. A college friend who also pastored churches in the same area wrote of their sleepy trips back to Birmingham well after midnight following weekends of serving their congregations. He also complimented Fr. Gordon's powerful preaching in revivals in their service area.

An Orthodox priest wrote to thank Fr. Gordon for his role in bringing this man's church and so many others into Orthodoxy. One man wrote to say that Fr. Gordon got him out of jail twice and helped him grow spiritually over several years. Another man who was converted in his twenties and is now a monk wrote to thank Fr. Gordon for introducing him to a personal God and for his emphasis on the virtue of humility, a virtue emphasized daily in his monastery.

Other writers described their interaction with him at meetings of Orthodox Christian Laity, an organization he loved and frequently assisted in their remarkable work for Orthodox unity. Still others wrote of their appreciation for his preaching and teaching in Campus Crusade and in conferences at the Antiochian Village.

THE MINISTRY OF FR. GORDON AND HIS FAMILY has cast a great circle of Christian love wherever they have lived and provided an excellent role model for all who have known them. As these letters testify, their ministry has concentrated on helping individuals, especially those most in need of the love of God. Above all, their lives are a testimony to the enduring truth of Orthodoxy, that pearl of great price for which Fr. Gordon sacrificed so many other high-profile opportunities for Christian service. May his memory be eternal!

Fr. Gordon with brother Phillip at Fr. Gordon's final Pascha in 2015

Future Plans

IN THE LAST FEW YEARS OF HIS LIFE, Fr. Gordon expressed his desire that some aspects of his ministry could survive into the future. In particular he hoped that the log house could be used as it had been used for many years, as a center of Christian hospitality dedicated to helping those in need of counseling and the influence of a Christian community.

Fr. Stephen Rogers has said that Fr. Gordon's ministry was "an inspiration to everyone." In particular, "his compassion for the individual" was paramount in his life and work. This book has attempted to display that commitment to individuals and their needs, but Fr. Gordon hoped that his concerns might be realized in a more direct, concrete manner.

That desire is now becoming a reality, as the log house has been transformed into the St. Thomas House (STH). The STH will continue to serve as a house of hospitality in support of many activities, including the following:

1. small group conferences;

2. priests and others visiting St. Ignatius; and

3. selected individuals with spiritual needs who may live in the home and who can benefit from in-house Bible studies and Christian fellowship.

The board of Grace Ministries continues to explore additional opportunities for Christian hospitality under the direction of our beloved Bp. Nicholas.

This is the kind of plan Fr. Gordon hoped to see develop at the log house. We pray that his commitment to the needs of individuals, and in particular their need to belong to a Christian community, will live on in the life of St. Thomas House.

The log house (St. Thomas House) in winter

Final Thoughts

These memoirs of Fr. Gordon Walker were written during the last few years of his life on earth. One of the biggest blessings to him in the writing of this book was the opportunity to bring to his memory so many people that he dearly loved. Many stories he told to the writer with warm tears in his eyes.

As with any life, there are hardships along with the good times. For many years Fr. Gordon had been afflicted with painful peripheral neuropathy in his legs resulting from his plane crash in Xenia, Ohio, as mentioned in this book. In his final years he endured the added affliction of slowly advancing Alzheimer's disease. As with all of the other challenges of his life, he trusted in the Lord and struggled to do his best for the benefit of others. Many of those closest to him realize that his desire to care for his true love, Mary Sue, was always in his heart and drove him to find the strength to do whatever was necessary.

Fr. Gordon was diagnosed with rapidly progressive metastatic prostate cancer in December, 2014, and died eight months later on July 23, 2015. Very fittingly, Fr. Gordon is buried in the little cemetery located on Grace Valley Farm next to St. Ignatius Antiochian Orthodox Christian Church. All are welcome to come and visit.

Before this book could be published, Mary Sue, who suffered from Alzheimer's disease, fell, broke her hip, and within a week had gone to be with her Lord and Savior Jesus Christ. She is buried beside Gordon, her partner in life and death.

Memory Eternal!